A SHORT
COURSE
IN BASIC

A SHORT COURSE IN BASIC

Problem Solving with Structure and Style

STEWART M. VENIT

California State University, Los Angeles

Composition: Parkwood Composition Service
Copyeditor: Janet M. Hunter
Cover design: Thomas W. Heffron
Cover image: *Folded Diamond #98* by Guy John Cavalli, Albany, CA
Text design: John Edeen

Several trademarks and/or service marks appear in this book. The companies listed below are the owners of the trademarks and/or service marks following their names.

Apple Computer, Inc.: Apple II, Applesoft BASIC, Macintosh
Commodore International Ltd.: Commodore 64
Digital Equipment Corporation: DEC, PDP-11, VAX-11, VAX-11 minicomputer
International Business Machines Corp.: IBM PC, IBM PC/AT, System 360
Microsoft Corporation: Microsoft BASIC
Tandy Corp.: TRS-80

COPYRIGHT © 1988 By WEST PUBLISHING COMPANY
50 W. Kellogg Boulevard
P.O. Box 64526
St. Paul, MN 55164-1003

Library of Congress Cataloging-in-Publication Data

Venit, Stewart.
    A short course in BASIC / Stewart M. Venit.
       p. cm.
    ISBN 0-314-62283-7
    1. BASIC (Computer program language)   I. Title.
QA76.73.B3V47   1988   87-21282
005. 13'3—dc 19   CIP

CONTENTS

CHAPTER 2 INPUT AND OUTPUT 28

CHAPTER 3 LOOPS 55

CHAPTER 4 DECISIONS 84

CHAPTER 5   MODULAR PROGRAMMING   110

CHAPTER 6   ARRAYS   129

CHAPTER 7   BASIC FUNCTIONS   148

PREFACE

PURPOSE

This text is intended for use in a short BASIC course for beginning students. In spite of its size, the text achieves two major goals: it teaches computer programming in general and the BASIC language in particular. We emphasize structured programming principles: problem solving, modular program design, structured coding, and programming style. Students using this text will learn to write readable, reliable and well-documented programs, and will be able to move on to other programming courses without having to unlearn bad habits.

VERSIONS OF BASIC

All programs in this text have been written using the IBM PC version of Microsoft BASIC. Nevertheless, the material is fairly generic, organized around programming concepts rather than language specifics. This is reflected in the chapter titles (for instance, Input and Output, Loops, and Decisions) as well as in their content. As an example, Do While and Do Until loops are introduced via IF...THEN and GOTO statements because these statements underscore the differences in structure between the two. Then, later in the same section, the combination of WHILE/WEND statements is brought forth as a better way (when available) to implement the Do While type of loop.

FEATURES

1. The text introduces the BASIC language quickly: the first program appears on the first page of the first chapter.

2. New statements are presented through short programs or program segments, avoiding at *this point*, elaborate program design and long explanations.

3. Structured programming principles are emphasized throughout the text.

4. All programs are written using good programming style. Style Pointers are highlighted throughout the text beginning in chapter 1.

5. The text contains detailed *applications*—longer programs illustrating the complete program development process of analysis, design, coding, and testing. (Most of these appear in the Focus on Problem Solving sections.) Program design is done using both pseudocode and flowcharts (with the aid of hierarchy charts for the modularized programs).

6. Review exercises are supplied at the end of each chapter. These include short answer, debugging, and skill builder exercises (answers to the odd-numbered ones are in appendix C). Programming problems, offering a wide range of difficulty, also appear at the end of each chapter.

7. Programming Pointers describing common programming errors and providing debugging tips appear throughout the text.

8. The organization of the text provides flexibility of use. The last three chapters are independent of one another, allowing an instructor to select from among many topics to fill out a course once the core material has been covered.

9. Although all programs are written in Microsoft BASIC, the text is generic enouch in nature to be used by those using other versions of BASIC. Differences among various dialects are highlighted throughout the text.

10. A quick reference guide to the BASIC statements and functions covered in the text is given on the inside covers.

SUPPLEMENT AVAILABLE

An *Instructor's Manual* is keyed to this text. It contains teaching suggestions, additional exercises (with answers), answers to the even-numbered Review Exercises, solutions to selected Progrmming Problems, and transparency masters for easy display or reproduction of important material.

ACKNOWLEDGMENTS

I would like to thank the many people who helped me bring this project to fruition. The following reviewers greatly improved the text through their thoughful comments and useful suggestions:

George Jacobson
Business Information Systems
California State University Los Angeles

Steve Scott
Computer Information Systems
Northeastern A&M College

Bernard Byrne
Mathematics
Castleton State College

Bernard Troy
Computer Education
California Polytechnic State University
San Luis Obispo

Pat Ormond
Data Processing
Utah Technical College

Virginia Mathie
Psychology
James Madison University

Blake Ashworth
Computer Instruction
L.H. Bates Voc/Tech

John Avitable
Computer Science
Rutgers University

Michael Dorey
Computer Technology
Brazosport College

I was fortunate to have Richard Jones as my editor. His many suggestions and helpful comments made this a better book. I am also indebted to Jan Hunter, who did the copyediting, and Bill Gabler, who guided the text through production. Finally, I would like to thank my wife, Corinne, and my daughter, Tamara, for their encouragement and support.

INTRODUCTION

Fifty years ago, electronic computers did not exist. Just twenty-five years ago, there were fewer than 25,000 of them. Today, millions of computers are in use around the world.

In their early days, computers were used almost exclusively by large businesses, engineering firms, universities and government institutions. At that time, they were expensive, somewhat tempermental machines, kept isolated in their own air-conditioned rooms and operated by specially trained personnel.

Today computers are everywhere. You can find them in homes, schools, and offices; in supermarkets and fast-food restaurants; and on airliners and space probes. They are used by the young and the old, by filmmakers and farmers, and by bankers and baseball managers. We use computers in almost limitless ways: for entertainment, education, money management, product design and manufacture, and to run our businesses and institutions. There are now few human endeavors that are not somehow touched by the use of the electronic computer.

In this introduction, we will discuss what the computer is and how it's used. Although you can certainly learn BASIC programming without reading this material, the background information provided here should help to increase your computer literacy.

THE COMPONENTS OF A COMPUTER

A **computer** is a mechanical or electronic device that can store, retrieve, and manipulate large amounts of information at high speed and with great accuracy. It can also act upon intermediate results without human intervention during execution of a task. The computer is able to perform its tasks without human intervention by carrying out (or *executing*) a list of instructions called a **program.**

To help you understand the workings of a computer, we will describe the components that make up a general *computer system*:

1. The central processing unit (CPU)

2. The primary storage unit

3. Secondary storage devices

4. Input devices

5. Output devices

This physical equipment is called computer **hardware.** Figure 1 illustrates the relationships among these components; the arrows show the direction of the flow of information.

The Central Processing Unit

The **central processing unit** (or **CPU**) is the brain of the computer. It consists of two major components.

1. A **control unit** which processes the instructions and directs the flow of information throughout the computer system.

2. An **arithmetic/logic unit** which performs the necessary arithmetic (addition, subtraction, and so on) and logical operations (like comparing two numbers).

In modern computers, the entire CPU often resides on a single *microchip,* a piece of silicon about the size of a postage stamp containing thousands of electronic components.

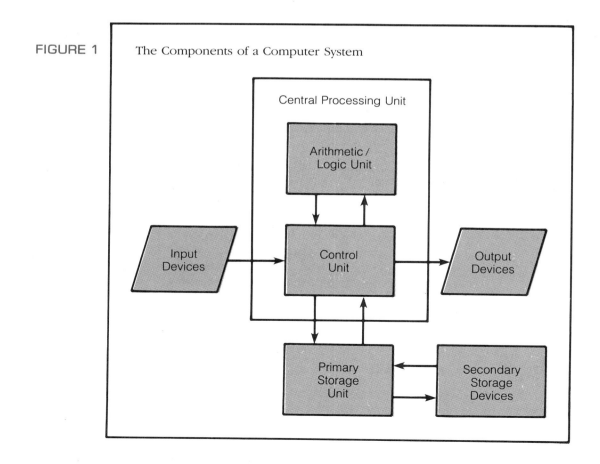

FIGURE 1 | The Components of a Computer System

The Primary Storage Unit

The **primary storage unit** stores the information to be processed by the CPU. This information consists of the program being executed, as well as the **data**—numbers, words, and other symbols—manipulated by it. The primary storage unit is known by several other names: **internal memory, main memory,** and **RAM** (for Random Access Memory).

In modern computers, the internal memory consists of a set of microchips connected by very fine wires. The CPU interacts with its primary storage unit at a very high rate of speed; it takes only a fraction of a millionth of a second for it to access memory. Unfortunately, any information stored there is lost when the computer's power is turned off.

Internal memory is partitioned into storage locations called **memory cells.** Each memory cell is capable of storing one **character** (letter, digit, comma, asterisk, and so on), also known as one **byte** of information. On most computers, one byte is made up of a combination of eight zeros and ones, each of which is called a **bit** (for binary digit).

One indication of the power of a computer is the number of storage locations it contains, the size of its internal memory. This number is usually expressed in *kilobytes* (KB), with one kilobyte equal to 1,024 ($= 2^{10}$) bytes. For example, an IBM PC with 256 KB of RAM contains 262,144 ($= 256 \times 1,024$) storage locations in its internal memory.

NOTE   We sometimes speak of the CPU and internal memory as being *the* computer. The secondary storage and input/output devices are referred to as **peripherals.** All these components taken together make up a **computer system.**

Secondary Storage Devices

Secondary storage is a form of computer memory used to hold a large amount of information semipermanently. Programs and data residing there can be erased if so desired, but unlike primary storage, they are *not* lost when the power is turned off. However, to use programs (or data) located in secondary storage, we must first *load* (transfer) them into the computer's internal memory.

In microcomputers, secondary storage usually takes the form of a **diskette** (or **floppy disk**), either 3½ or 5¼ inches in diameter. To load a program into a microcomputer, you simply insert the diskette into its **disk drive** (the secondary storage *device*) and type the appropriate characters at the keyboard. On some microcomputers and virtually all larger machines, secondary storage resides on a **hard disk,** permanently mounted in its disk drive. (Hard disks store more information and transfer it more quickly than diskettes.) To load a program contained on a hard disk, we just type the appropriate characters at the keyboard.

Input Devices

An **input device** enables us to communicate with the computer. It accepts information in a form that is understandable to people (such as typed or spoken words), transforms it into a machine readable form, and transmits it to the computer.

The typewriter-like **keyboard** is by far the most common input device in use today. To enter information into the computer, you simply type it at the keyboard in much the same way you would if you were using an ordinary typewriter. (Computer keyboards contain a few more keys than a typewriter; the extra ones facilitate communication with the machine.)

Another type of input device is used to "point" at items on the display screen, and thus initiate an action. The most popular of these is the *mouse,* a small object containing one or two buttons, that moves a pointer on the screen when you roll it around on the desktop. Pointing devices, such as the mouse, can speed up some input operations, but they lack the versatility of the keyboard.

Output Devices

An **output device** enables the computer to "talk" to us; it transmits information from the machine to the outside world in a form understandable to humans. This is usually done by means of a *video monitor* or a *printer.*

A video **monitor** is a television-like device also known as a **display screen,** **CRT** (for Cathode Ray Tube), or **VDT** (for Video Display Terminal). Monitors, like TVs, come in color or "black and white" (monochrome) models. (Monochrome monitors usually display green or amber characters on a black background.)

To make a permanent copy (or **hard copy**) of the computer's output on paper, we use a **printer.** These come in several varieties including *daisywheel* printers, which produce characters like those of an expensive typewriter, and *dot matrix* printers, whose characters (and graphics) are made up of many tiny dots. The daisywheel's output has greater clarity than that of most dot matrix printers, but the daisywheel does not have the versatility or speed of the dot matrix. The *laser* printer combines the print quality of the daisywheel with the speed of the fastest dot matrix printer. Unfortunately, laser printers are far more expensive than either of the other two types.

A typical microcomputer system is shown in figure 2.

TYPES OF COMPUTERS

The computer market today comprises a vast array of machines. The smallest and least expensive computers are called **microcomputers,** or **personal computers.** They are roughly the size of an office typewriter and range in price from less than $100 to about $5,000. Their names have become household words: Apple II, Commodore 64, IBM PC, Macintosh, and so on. Although *micros* are small and inexpensive, they pack a remarkable amount of computing power. A typical microcomputer is as powerful as a state-of-the-art computer of the mid-1960s, a machine that was hundreds of times its size and cost.

Somewhat larger, more expensive, and more powerful computers are called **minicomputers.** These machines, unlike personal computers, can be used by a number of people (typically 16 to 32) working simultaneously at separate remote

FIGURE 2   The IBM PC/AT (Courtesy of International Business Machines Corporation)

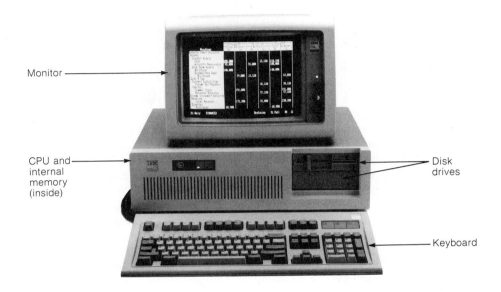

Monitor

CPU and
internal
memory
(inside)

Disk
drives

Keyboard

terminals. Minicomputers have become the mainstay of relatively small businesses and universities. They range in price from about $20,000 to $300,000. At the upper end of this price range, the **superminicomputers** rival the computing power of mainframes.

The most powerful computers are called **mainframes.** These relatively large and costly ($500,000 to $15,000,000) machines supply their users with unsurpassed power to manipulate information. For a large oil company or the Internal Revenue Service, there is no substitute for a mainframe. The most powerful (and expensive) of the mainframes are called **supercomputers.** The fastest supercomputers can now process about one billion instructions per second.

PROGRAMMING LANGUAGES

The computer's hardware (its CPU, memory, and peripherals) is useless without instructions that tell it what to do. The first computers were given these instructions (the *program*) by actually rewiring some of their circuits. Needless to say, this was a painstaking task. Then, in the late 1940s, the great mathematician John von Neumann came up with the idea of storing the program in the computer's internal memory, and this is the way it has been done ever since.

Types of Programming Languages

A **programming language** is a set of symbols, and the rules governing their use, employed in constructing programs. Programming languages are of three fundamental types:

1. Machine languages

2. Assembly languages

3. High-level languages

A **machine language** program consists of a sequence of zeros and ones. The numbers specified, and the order in which they appear, tell the computer what to do. Machine language, which differs considerably from one type of computer to another, is the only language the machine can understand directly. However, as you might imagine, it is very difficult for humans to read or write. For this reason, **programmers** write their programs in either *assembly* or *high-level* languages.

Assembly language is a symbolic representation of machine language. There is usually a one-to-one correspondence between the two; each assembly language instruction translates into one machine language instruction. However, assembly language uses easily recognizable codes, which make it a lot easier for people to understand. For example, the following instructions add two numbers on a DEC PDP-11 computer:

Machine Language Instruction:
    0110110111110111 0000000000000010 0000000000000010
Assembly Language Equivalent:
    ADD   A, B

Before a computer can carry out an assembly language program, it must be translated (by the computer) into machine language. This is done by a special program called an **assembler.**

High-level languages usually contain English words and phrases; their symbols and structure are far removed from those of machine language. High-level languages have several advantages over assembly language. They are easier to learn and use, and the resultant programs are easier to read and modify. A single instruction in a high-level language usually translates into many instructions in machine language. Moreover, a given high-level language does not differ much from computer to computer; a program written on one machine can usually be used on another with relatively few changes.

On the negative side, programs written in a high-level language are usually less efficient than their assembly language counterparts. High-level languages, like assembly languages, must be translated into machine language before their instructions can be carried out. This is done by programs known as *interpreters* and *compilers.*

The first high-level language, FORTRAN (which stands for FORmula TRANslation), was developed in the mid-1950s for engineering and scientific applications. Since then, there has been a flood of high-level languages. A few of these are

Ada (named after a nineteenth century Englishwoman, Ada Augusta Byron)—for military applications

APL (A Programming Language)—for scientific programming

BASIC (Beginner's All-purpose Symbolic Instruction Code)

COBOL (COmmon Business-Oriented Language)—for business-related programming

Pascal (named after Blaise Pascal, a seventeenth century philosopher and mathematician)—primarily for teaching programming concepts

BASIC

BASIC is the programming language you will learn in this book. It was created by John Kemeny and Thomas Kurtz at Dartmouth College in the mid-1960s for the specific purpose of providing students with a powerful, yet easy to learn, means of writing programs. Since the advent of microcomputers, which are often sold with BASIC included as part of the package, it has become the most popular programming language in use today.

As its popularity increased, so did the number of BASIC **dialects,** slightly different versions of the language. In 1978, the American National Standards Institute (ANSI) published a set of standards that defined a minimal form of this language. Virtually all BASIC dialects now contain minimal BASIC as their core. The most popular version of BASIC in use today is the one published by Microsoft Corporation, which is available for most microcomputers. In this book, we will emphasize Microsoft BASIC as well as a generic BASIC based upon the 1978 ANSI standard. We will also highlight the differences among these dialects and several others.

BASIC is usually translated into machine language by means of a program called an *interpreter.* The **interpreter** carries out each instruction of your program immediately after it has been translated. (A **compiler,** on the other hand, translates the entire program before carrying out any of the instructions.) As a result, it is possible to have the computer *execute* partial BASIC programs. This will enable you to see how your program is working before you complete it, if you so desire. The disadvantage of interpreted programs is that they execute considerably more slowly than their compiled counterparts.

REVIEW EXERCISES

1. In your own words, what is a computer?

2. According to your definition (exercise 1), which of the following qualify as computers:

   a. Simple calculators

   b. Programmable calculators

   c. Microwave ovens

   d. Digital watches

3. According to the definition given in the text, which of the items in exercise 2 are computers?

4. Name the three general types of computers. Give characteristics (size, cost, and so on) of each one.

5. Name the five major components of a computer system.

6. How many characters can be stored by a computer that has:

   a. 16 KB of RAM   b. 64 KB of RAM

7. Why are *both* primary and secondary storage necessary in a computer system?

8. Give one advantage of

   a. a daisywheel printer over a dot matrix printer.
   b. a dot matrix printer over a daisywheel printer.

9. Name the three general categories of computer languages.

10. What is one advantage of

    a. an assembly language over a high-level language?
    b. a high-level language over an assembly language?

THE BASICS
OF BASIC

In this chapter you will learn how to write simple BASIC programs. We will discuss some fundamental concepts of the BASIC language as well as the general process for transforming a given problem into a usable program. This chapter also introduces the important notion of programming style.

1.1   A SIMPLE BASIC PROGRAM

A **program** is simply a list of instructions to the computer to perform some task. BASIC, which stands for *Beginners' All-purpose Symbolic Instruction Code,* is a simple, yet powerful, language for writing programs. In a BASIC program, each instruction, or **statement,** begins with an English word, known as a **keyword.** Even to a nonprogrammer, the meaning of a BASIC program is often easy to understand. The following simple program illustrates this point:

EXAMPLE 1.1
```
100 REM   **   OUR FIRST PROGRAM!   **
110 REM   S. VENIT          JANUARY, 1987
120 REM
130     PRINT "HELLO, OUT THERE!"
140     PRINT "GOODBYE."
150     END
```

To **execute** this program (that is, to have the computer carry out its instructions), we first have to **enter** it into the computer's internal memory. This is done

1

by typing the **lines** of the program, exactly as they appear in example 1.1, at the keyboard. (The Enter key, which may be labeled "Enter", "Return", or "←⏐", must be pressed at the end of each line.) Once the program has been entered, we can execute it by typing the word RUN and pressing the Enter key. The computer will then carry out the program's instructions. (We will discuss the process of entering and executing a program in more detail in section 1.5.)

When the program in example 1.1 is executed, the following two lines will be displayed on the screen:

```
HELLO, OUT THERE!
GOODBYE.
```

NOTE The data displayed on the screen or printed after a program is executed are called the **output** of the program. The display of the program lines themselves (or program **code**) is called a **listing** of the program.

Let's take a closer look at our first program. Each line consists of a number—the **line number**—followed by a BASIC statement. For example, the fifth line of our program is

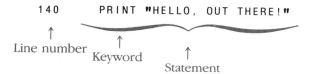

```
140        PRINT "HELLO, OUT THERE!"
```

Line number   Keyword   Statement

(From now on, for simplicity's sake, we will refer to "statement xxx" rather than "the statement in line xxx.")

Line numbers serve the following purposes in BASIC programs:

1. They give the order in which the lines appear.

2. They are an aid in modifying the program (see appendix A).

3. They provide labels for the statements.

The REM Statement

The first three statements of the program in example 1.1

```
100 REM   **   OUR FIRST PROGRAM!   **
110 REM   S. VENIT        JANUARY, 1987
120 REM
```

are known as REM statements, or **remarks** or **comments.** These statements are placed in a program to **document** it, to supply commentary for someone *reading* the program. They are not for someone *executing* or *using* it, for when the program is executed, the listing cannot be seen by the user.

The first two REM statements in our example (lines 100 and 110) identify the program's title, its programmer, and the date the program was created. The third REM statement (line 120) provides a blank line (well, almost a blank line) for the sake of legibility.

When the computer encounters the keyword REM at the beginning of a statement, it ignores the rest of that statement and moves on to the next one. We say that REMs are **non-executable statements;** they declare information rather than demand action. Remember: Comments are for the person reading the program, not for the computer executing it. The proper use of REM statements is a key ingredient in developing a good programming style (as we'll see in section 1.6).

The REM statement

Form   REM [Your comment here.]
              or
              REM [No comment included, just a blank space.]

Purpose   To document the program for its human reader.

Example   `200 REM    THIS PROGRAM DOES VIRTUALLY NOTHING.`

The PRINT Statement

When the PRINT statements in our program

```
130       PRINT "HELLO, OUT THERE!"
140       PRINT "GOODBYE."
```

are executed, the message, or **text,** between the quotation marks is displayed on the screen. These statements create the program's output:

```
HELLO, OUT THERE!
GOODBYE.
```

Whereas REM statements provide information to those *reading* the program, PRINT statements result in the display of information for those *using* the program. They are **executable statements,** causing an action (the display of data) to take place. The PRINT statement described here is a simple version of a very powerful BASIC statement.

The PRINT statement (first form)

Form   PRINT "text"

Action   Displays the text between the quotation marks.

Example   `350   PRINT "WELCOME TO THE PROGRAM!"`

We will discuss the PRINT statement further in sections 1.2, 1.3, and 2.4.

PROGRAMMING POINTER

A PRINT statement will display whatever text appears between the quotation marks, whether or not it makes any sense. This includes any blanks resulting from pressing the space bar on the keyboard. For example, when the code

```
400      PRINT "***"
410      PRINT "   ***"
```

is executed,

```
***
   ***
```

is displayed.

You will see more Programming Pointers throughout the text. In them, we give tips on preventing common programming errors.

The END Statement

The last statement in a BASIC program is the END statement. It is a signal to the computer to halt execution. We also use it to indicate the physical end of a program.

The END statement

Form   END

Action   Terminates program execution.

Example   `360    END`

1.2   THE LET STATEMENT; CONSTANTS AND VARIABLES

Our first BASIC program (example 1.1) just printed text (messages). The next one manipulates numbers as well.

EXAMPLE 1.2

```
100 REM    ********   PROGRAM 2   ********
110 REM    S. VENIT            JANUARY, 1987
120 REM
130 REM    THIS PROGRAM ILLUSTRATES THE LET STATEMENT AND
140 REM    PRESENTS NUMERIC CONSTANTS AND VARIABLES.
150 REM
160        LET A = 10.6
170        LET B = -1.5
180        LET B = A
190        PRINT "THE VALUE OF A IS"
200        PRINT A
210        PRINT "THE VALUE OF B IS"
220        PRINT B
230        END
```

The LET (Assignment) Statement

As in example 1.1, the first two REM statements identify the program, the programmer, and the date. Additionally, those in lines 130 and 140 state the *purpose* of the program.

The statement

```
160        LET A = 10.6
```

is called an **assignment** (or LET) **statement.** It assigns the value 10.6 to the variable A. A **variable** in a BASIC program is a quantity that can change its value during program execution. The statement

```
170        LET B = -1.5
```

assigns the value -1.5 to the variable B.

The next line in the program,

```
180        LET B = A
```

causes the value of A (10.6) to be assigned to the variable B. Thus, B takes on a new value, 10.6, while that of A remains unchanged.

**Whenever a new value is assigned to a variable,
it replaces the previous value (if any).**

We can illustrate the action of statements 160, 170, and 180 by means of a **trace table.** The entry in table 1.1 under B denoted by the dash indicates that B has not yet been assigned a value at this point; it remains an **undefined variable** until line 170.

TABLE 1.1   A TRACE TABLE FOR EXAMPLE 1.2

STATEMENT	A	B
160 LET A = 10.6	10.6	—
170 LET B = −1.5	10.6	−1.5
180 LET B = A	10.6	10.6

In most versions of BASIC, if a variable is used before it is assigned a value in the program, it will automatically be set equal to 0. For example, if the first statement of a program is

    100   LET C = D

then both C and D will have value 0 after that statement is executed.

The LET (assignment) statement (first form)

Form   LET variable = constant
            or
            LET variable1 = variable2

Action   Sets the variable on the left of the equal sign equal to the constant or variable value on the right.

Examples   220   LET X = 86.3
            310   LET X = Y

PROGRAMMING POINTER

If a variable appears to the right of the equal sign in a LET statement, it should have been assigned a value earlier in the program; it should *not* be an undefined variable.

Numeric Constants and Variables

A **numeric constant** is just BASIC's name for a number. In example 1.2, 10.6 and −1.5 are numeric constants, or more simply, constants. In BASIC, we write constants the same way we write numbers in mathematics, but with one major exception: commas are not permitted in constants. (See table 1.2.)

TABLE 1.2   SOME VALID AND INVALID BASIC CONSTANTS

VALID	INVALID
2341456	2,341,456
4.53	$4.53
—0.35	—35d100

Since the variables A and B in example 1.2 represent numbers, they are called **numeric variables.** As far as the computer is concerned, a variable is the name given to a location in its internal (main) memory. When a value is assigned to a variable, that number is stored in a location in memory identified by the variable name.

Although the symbols that can be used to represent a variable vary depending upon the version (or **dialect**) of BASIC that you are using, there is common ground here (see tables 1.3 and 1.4).

In all versions of BASIC, numeric variables may be represented by either a single letter or a single letter immediately followed by a single digit (0 through 9).

TABLE 1.3   ALLOWABLE VARIABLE NAMES IN BASIC

COMPUTER	CHARACTERS ALLOWED*	NUMBER ALLOWED
Apple II Commodore 64 TRS-80	Letters, digits	Any number, but computer recognizes only the first 2
IBM PC Macintosh	Letters, digits, periods	Any number, but computer recognizes only the first 40
VAX-11	Letters, digits, underscores	A maximum of 29

*The first character must be a letter.

TABLE 1.4   SOME VALID AND INVALID BASIC VARIABLE NAMES

VALID	INVALID
X	7B (Must begin with a letter)
A1	R 5 (No blanks allowed)
B0	A@ (@ not a legal character)
Z9	
PRICE (Valid in most dialects)	
TEST1 (Valid in most dialects)	

Returning to example 1.2, the next few lines are

```
190      PRINT "THE VALUE OF A IS"
200      PRINT A
210      PRINT "THE VALUE OF B IS"
220      PRINT B
```

Statements 190 and 210 print the given messages (as in example 1.1), but statements 200 and 220 act differently. Here, the word PRINT is followed by a program variable, not by a phrase contained within quotation marks. Upon execution, statement 200 prints the current value of A, namely 10.6, and statement 220 prints that of B, also 10.6. Thus, the output of the program is

```
THE VALUE OF A IS
 10.6
THE VALUE OF B IS
 10.6
```

More on PRINT

The output of example 1.2 looks somewhat awkward. It would be nicer if each number displayed appeared on the same line as the text identifying it. We can accomplish this by placing both of these items in the same PRINT statement separated by a semicolon; that is, by changing lines 190 and 210 to read

```
190      PRINT "THE VALUE OF A IS"; A
210      PRINT "THE VALUE OF B IS"; B
```

and deleting lines 200 and 220 from the program. Now the output is

```
THE VALUE OF A IS 10.6
THE VALUE OF B IS 10.6
```

> If a semicolon is placed between items listed in a PRINT statement, the items will be displayed on the same line, one immediately following the other.

NOTE   In most forms of BASIC, all printed numbers are followed by a space (a *trailing blank*) and positive numbers are preceded by a space (a *leading blank*). This often leads to unexpected spacing of output. For example, the code

```
200      LET A = 1
210      LET B = —1
220      PRINT "NUMBERS"; A; "AND"; B
```

produces the output

```
NUMBERS 1 AND—1
```

The space before the 1 is a leading blank and the space after it is a trailing blank. There is no leading blank before the −1 because it is negative.

PROGRAMMING POINTER

Whenever you print a numeric expression preceded by a message, place a blank at the end of the message, unless you are sure that the value of the expression will *never* be negative. For example

```
430      PRINT "THE VALUE IS "; X
```
                              ↑
                              └──────────── Blank

Normally, after execution of a PRINT statement, a carriage return takes place. This causes the next PRINT statement to display its text (or variable values) beginning in the first position of the next line. If you want to prevent this from happening—if you want to suppress the carriage return—place a semicolon at the end of the PRINT list.

EXAMPLE 1.3   This example shows why it is sometimes desirable to suppress the carriage return.

```
500      PRINT "THE OUTPUT PRODUCED BY THESE TWO STATEMENTS";
510      PRINT "WILL APPEAR ON ONE LONG LINE"
```

Due to the semicolon at the end of statement 500, no carriage return takes place. As a result, statements 500 and 510 print on the same line. The output is

```
THE OUTPUT PRODUCED BY THESE TWO STATEMENTSWILL APPEAR ON ONE LONG LINE
```

Notice that the words STATEMENTS and WILL run together. This occurs because the semicolon suppressing the carriage return also causes printing to resume immediately following the last character displayed. To correct the situation, place a blank just before the second quotation mark in line 500.

```
500      PRINT "THE OUTPUT PRODUCED BY THESE TWO STATEMENTS ";
```

The PRINT statement revisited

Form   PRINT item; item; . . . ; item [;]
where the word *item* represents a variable or text enclosed in quotation marks; the brackets around the final semicolon—[;]—indicate that this semicolon is optional.

Action   Prints the value of the items one after the other, then causes a carriage return unless the statement ends with a semicolon.

Examples
```
320      PRINT A; "OKEY "; "DOKEY";
540      PRINT X; "AND "; Y
```

We close this section with an important warning.

PROGRAMMING POINTER

If a variable appears in a PRINT statement, it should have been assigned a value earlier in the program; it must *not* be an undefined variable. If you print the value of such a variable, either an *error message* or the number 0 will be displayed, depending upon your version of BASIC. This kind of error is often caused by typing mistakes. For example, it occurs when the following statements are executed:

```
200      LET PROFIT = 1000
210      PRINT PRIFIT
```

PROFIT is misspelled in line 210; hence, as far as the computer is concerned, it is an undefined variable.

1.3 ARITHMETIC OPERATIONS

The next program illustrates how we can perform addition, subtraction, multiplication, and division using BASIC.

EXAMPLE 1.4

```
100 REM    ***  ARITHMETIC OPERATIONS  ***
110 REM    S. VENIT              JANUARY, 1987
120 REM
130 REM    THIS PROGRAM ADDS, SUBTRACTS, MULTIPLIES,
140 REM    AND DIVIDES THE TWO GIVEN NUMBERS.
150 REM
160 REM    VARIABLES:
170 REM       X, Y .......... THE GIVEN NUMBERS
180 REM       SUM, DIFF ..... THEIR SUM AND DIFFERENCE
190 REM       PROD, QUOT .... THEIR PRODUCT AND QUOTIENT
200 REM
210        LET X = 5
220        LET Y = 3
230        PRINT "ARITHMETIC OPERATIONS WILL BE PERFORMED ON:"
240        PRINT X; "AND "; Y
250 REM
260 REM      COMPUTE SUM, DIFFERENCE, PRODUCT, QUOTIENT
270 REM
280        LET SUM = X + Y
290        LET DIFF = X — Y
300        LET PROD = X * Y
310        LET QUOT = X / Y
320 REM
330 REM      PRINT RESULTS
340 REM
350        PRINT "THE SUM IS "; SUM
360        PRINT "THE DIFFERENCE IS "; DIFF
370        PRINT "THE PRODUCT IS "; PROD
380        PRINT "THE QUOTIENT IS "; QUOT
390 REM
400        END
```

Statements 280–310 perform the calculations. In each case, when the LET statement is executed, the value of the expression to the right of the equal sign is computed (the expression is *evaluated*) and this value is assigned to the variable on the left. These values are then printed in statements 350–380, producing the output

```
THE SUM IS  8
THE DIFFERENCE IS  2
THE PRODUCT IS  15
THE QUOTIENT IS  1.666667
```

NOTE   The blank spaces before and after the operator symbols ($+$, $-$, $*$, and $/$) in lines 280–310 of example 1.4 are not required. They do, however, improve program readability.

BASIC also provides a symbol for *exponentiation,* the operation of raising a number to a power. Recall that in mathematics,

$$2^4 = 2 \times 2 \times 2 \times 2 = 16 \text{ and } 5^3 = 5 \times 5 \times 5 = 125.$$

More generally, if n is a positive integer, then

$$a^n = \underbrace{(a)(a)\dots(a)}_{n \text{ factors}}$$

The BASIC symbol for exponentiation is a caret (^). An up arrow (↑) is also used for this purpose, but ^ is more common on computer keyboards.

EXAMPLE 1.5   The following program segment computes the value of 17 taken to the third, fourth, and fifth power:

```
520      LET T = 17
530      LET T3 = T ^ 3
540      LET T4 = T ^ 4
550      LET T5 = T ^ 5
```

Table 1.5 summarizes the BASIC symbols for the arithmetic operations discussed here.

TABLE 1.5   BASIC OPERATION SYMBOLS

SYMBOL	OPERATION	EXAMPLE	MEANING
$+$	Addition	A + 9.1	Add value of A and 9.1
$-$	Subtraction	6 − B	Subtract value of B from 6
$*$	Multiplication	5 * (−3)	Multiply 5 and −3
/	Division	C / C1	Divide value of C by C1
^	Exponentiation	5 ^ 4	Take 5 to the fourth power

PROGRAMMING POINTER

> Two consecutive operation symbols are not permitted. For example, $5 * -3$ is not valid; you should use either $5 * (-3)$ or $-3 * 5$.

Numeric Expressions

In the examples you have seen so far, the BASIC arithmetic operators have been used in a limited way: they have appeared in expressions containing only two constants and/or variables. In fact, these operators can be used to form expressions of any type that is valid in ordinary algebra. Since the value of these expressions is a number, they are called **numeric expressions.**

EXAMPLE 1.6

Determine the value of X after the following BASIC statement is executed. Assume that the values of A and B are 9 and 6, respectively.

```
200    LET X = (2 * (A + 3)) - ((B / 2) ^ 3)
```

To evaluate this expression, we first replace A by 9 and B by 6 and then perform the indicated operations according to the rules of arithmetic.

$$
\begin{aligned}
&(2 * (A + 3)) - ((B / 2) \char`\^ 3) \\
&= (2 * (9 + 3)) - ((6 / 2) \char`\^ 3) \\
&= (2 * 12) - (3 \char`\^ 3) \\
&= 24 - 27 \\
&= -3
\end{aligned}
$$

The number -3 is then assigned to X.

In example 1.6, the order in which the operations are to be performed is made clear by the use of parentheses. In the absence of parentheses, the following rules (which are the same as those of arithmetic) govern the order. Of course, if parentheses *do* appear, the expressions within them must be evaluated first.

Hierarchy of arithmetic operations

Expressions in parentheses are evaluated first.
Exponentiations are done next.
Multiplications and divisions are done next.
In a sequence of multiplications and divisions, the operations are done from left to right.
Additions and subtractions are done last.
In a sequence of additions and subtractions, the operations are done from left to right.

EXAMPLE 1.7   Evaluate the following BASIC expression.

$$4 / 2 * 3 \wedge 2 + 7 * 5 - 8$$

$$
\begin{aligned}
& \quad 4 / 2 * 3 \wedge 2 + 7 * 5 - 8 \\
&= 4 / 2 * 9 + 7 * 5 - 8 \\
&= 2 * 9 + 7 * 5 - 8 \\
&= 18 + 35 - 8 \\
&= 53 - 8 \\
&= 45
\end{aligned}
$$

(exponentiation first)
(multiplications and divisions
next, left to right)
(additions and subtractions
last, left to right)

The LET statement revisited

Form   LET variable = expression

Action   Evaluates the expression and assigns its value to the variable.

Example   `600   LET Z3 = (A + 7.2) ^ 3 - 17.1`

Printing Numeric Expressions

If we need to evaluate a numeric expression and display the result, we can do this in two steps by using a LET statement to perform the evaluation and a PRINT statement to print the result. For example, the following program segment computes the average of X, Y, and Z and displays this number:

```
350     LET AVG = (X + Y + Z) / 3
360     PRINT AVG
```

BASIC also allows us to perform these operations using just a PRINT statement:

```
350     PRINT (X + Y + Z) / 3
```

Here, the expression

$$(X + Y + Z) / 3$$

is evaluated and the resultant number is displayed. With this method, however, the value of the average is not available for use later in the program.

EXAMPLE 1.8   Write a single statement that

a. Computes and prints the sum of the squares of X and Y.

b. Computes and prints the area of a triangle with base equal to B and altitude equal to H.

For a.: 500   PRINT X ^ 2 + Y ^ 2
For b.: 500   PRINT B * H / 2

1.4   DESIGNING BASIC PROGRAMS

In the first three sections, you have seen several BASIC programs. In the next two sections, we will discuss the general process by which you can transform a given problem into a suitable BASIC program for solving it. Of course, in some sense this is the subject matter of the entire text, so we will have much more to say about this topic in later chapters.

The Program Development Cycle

In writing a computer program to solve a problem, we follow some general problem-solving principles. We must completely understand the problem, devise a plan to solve it, carry out that plan, and finally, review the results to make sure that we have in fact solved the given problem. When this process is applied to program writing, it means carrying out the following tasks:

1. Analyze the problem. (Make sure you understand it.)

2. Design the program. (Devise a plan to solve it.)

3. Code the program. (Carry out your plan.)

4. Test the program. (Review the results.)

This process is called the **program development cycle.** (Since another name for computer programs is **software,** it is also called the *software development cycle.*) The word "cycle" is used because we often have to return to previous steps and make modifications before the process is completed. For example, in the testing phase, we may find errors in the design process which require us to redesign the program, recode it, and retest it. In fact, in commercial programs, the cycle is rarely ever complete. Programs are continually evaluated and modified to meet changing demands or increasing competition.

We will now consider each of the steps in the program development cycle in greater detail and illustrate them in an example.

EXAMPLE 1.9   John Brewster has just inherited $4,500. He decides to place the money in a two-year certificate of deposit paying 9.6 percent interest, compounded quarterly. What will be the value of John's investment after the two years have passed?

Analyzing the Problem

First, we must study the problem until we completely understand it. We ask ourselves

1. What results are we trying to obtain: what is the required *output*?

2. What data are given: what is the *input* supplied?

3. Do we have enough information to obtain the required output from the given input?

At this stage, we choose variables to represent the given input and required output. We also start thinking about what formulas or logical processes we will have to carry out in order to get the desired results. In this way, our analysis of the problem will lead us naturally into the second step of the cycle, that of designing the program.

For example 1.9, the required output is the amount of money in the certificate after two years. The given inputs are the initial amount ($4,500), the interest rate (9.6 percent), the frequency of compounding (four times per year), and the period of the investment (two years). We now assign variables to these items.
Input Variables.
    P: initial amount
    R: interest rate
    N: number of times per year that compounding takes place
    T: number of years the money is invested
Output Variables.
    A: value of the investment after two years
To obtain the result, we use the compound interest formula, $A = P(1 + R/N)^{NT}$. Here, the rate of interest, R, must be given as a decimal, not a percentage.

Designing the Program

In this step, we devise an outline of our program; we construct a framework on which to build our code. This outline is like the one you would prepare before writing an essay for an English or history class.

In designing the program, we give a step-by-step procedure for solving the problem. Such a process is called an **algorithm.** (The resultant computer program can be considered a very detailed way of further describing this algorithm.) Algorithms abound in mathematics and are common in everyday life as well. For example, when we follow a recipe or use a bank's electronic teller, we are carrying out algorithms.

There are several standard formats for presenting the design of a program. Two of the most popular are flowcharts and pseudocode. A **flowchart** gives a pictorial representation of the design through *processing symbols* such as those in figure 1.1. (We will present additional flowcharting symbols later in the text as the need arises.) Flowcharts are also excellent tools for showing the structure of some BASIC statements and blocks of code.

Pseudocode closely resembles the outlining process familiar from essay writing. Here, short English-like phrases are used to describe the design. In this text, we will use pseudocode as the primary design tool, but we will usually provide flowcharts as well.

We will illustrate each of these methods of design by returning to example 1.9. In using pseudocode we have to ask ourselves what fundamental tasks we have

FIGURE 1.1

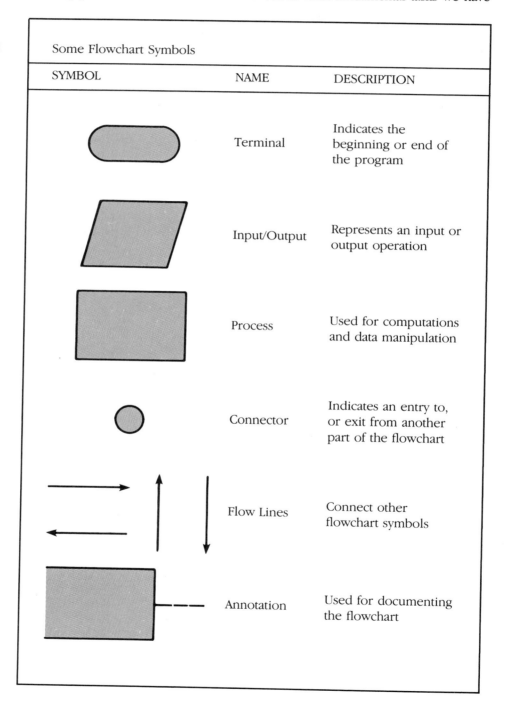

Some Flowchart Symbols

SYMBOL	NAME	DESCRIPTION
	Terminal	Indicates the beginning or end of the program
	Input/Output	Represents an input or output operation
	Process	Used for computations and data manipulation
	Connector	Indicates an entry to, or exit from another part of the flowchart
	Flow Lines	Connect other flowchart symbols
	Annotation	Used for documenting the flowchart

to perform in order to create the program. For our given problem, these tasks are

1. Assign the given data to the variables (P, R, N, and T).

2. Compute the final amount (A) by using the compound interest formula.

3. Print the value of A.

The flowchart for this program is given in figure 1.2. It describes the same algorithm for solving the problem, but in a pictorial fashion.

Notice that the structure of this program consists of three blocks: an assignment block, a computation block, and an output block. All of the programs that you write for a while will be of this simple form. However, as the programs become increasingly more complex, the need for a detailed design will become greater and greater.

FIGURE 1.2

The Flowchart for Example 1.9

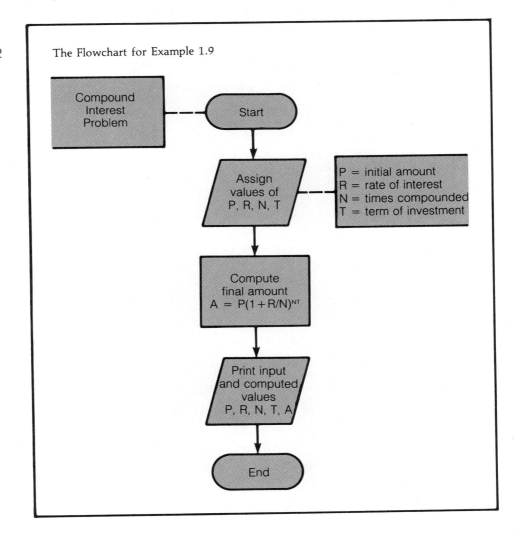

1.5   CODING AND TESTING BASIC PROGRAMS

In section 1.4, we began a discussion of the program development cycle, the process of solving a given problem by writing a suitable program. In this section, we will continue this discussion.

Coding the Program

We now sit down and, using the design as an outline, write the statements (or *code*) for the program on a sheet of lined paper (or a special coding form, if one is available). Notice that the design of the program makes no mention of comments (REM statements). These are written at this point in the programming process, together with the rest of the code. (Section 1.6 provides more information concerning the use of comments.)

Following the program design created for example 1.9, we write the code.

```
100 REM   **    BREWSTER'S THOUSANDS   **
110 REM
120 REM   S. VENIT            JANUARY, 1987
130 REM
140 REM   THIS PROGRAM COMPUTES THE VALUE OF AN INVESTMENT
150 REM   USING THE COMPOUND INTEREST FORMULA:
160 REM       A = P * (1 + R / N) ^ (N * T)
170 REM
180 REM   VARIABLES:
190 REM       P ... INITIAL AMOUNT OF THE INVESTMENT
200 REM       R ... ANNUAL INTEREST RATE (AS A DECIMAL)
210 REM       N ... FREQUENCY OF COMPOUNDING (TIMES PER YEAR)
220 REM       T ... PERIOD OF THE INVESTMENT (IN YEARS)
230 REM       A ... VALUE OF INVESTMENT AT END OF PERIOD
240 REM
250 REM   INPUT BLOCK
260 REM
270       LET P = 4500
280       LET R = 0.096
290       LET N = 4
300       LET T = 2
310 REM
320 REM   COMPUTATION BLOCK
330 REM
340       LET A = P * (1 + R / N) ^ (N * T)
350 REM
360 REM   OUTPUT BLOCK
370 REM
380       PRINT "THE VALUE OF AN INVESTMENT OF"; P; "DOLLARS"
390       PRINT "INVESTED AT A RATE OF"; R * 100; "PERCENT"
400       PRINT "COMPOUNDED"; N; "TIMES PER YEAR"
410       PRINT "FOR"; T; "YEARS IS"
420       PRINT A; "DOLLARS."
430 REM
440       END
```

After we write the program code, we check it for errors and make any necessary corrections. It is then time to enter it into the computer's internal memory.

Entering and Listing a Program

After you write your program on paper, you must enter it: transmit it to the computer's internal memory. To do this, you first have to establish communication with your computer and its *BASIC interpreter*, the software that translates your program into a form the computer can "understand." This process varies from computer to computer.

Once you are in BASIC, you enter the program by typing it at the computer (or terminal) keyboard. When typing it, be sure to end each line with a carriage return by pressing the Enter key. (As we saw before, this key will be labeled "Enter", "Return", or "←⏎", depending on the keyboard.) Pressing the Enter key does two things:

1. It transmits the program line to the computer's internal memory.

2. It moves the **cursor,** the little block of light showing the current typing location, to the left end of the next line.

After you have entered your program, it is a good idea to check it for typing errors. This can be done most easily by *listing* it: displaying the entire program (in the order given by the line numbers) as it appears in memory.

**To list a program, type the word LIST (at the beginning
of a new line) and press the Enter key.**

LIST is an example of a **system command,** an instruction to the computer to do something to the program. It is not preceded by a line number and does not become part of the program.

The easiest way to find program errors is to list your program on a printer, to make a **hard copy** of it. This is done by typing the command appropriate for your BASIC system (table 1.6) and pressing Enter.

TABLE 1.6   LISTING A PROGRAM ON THE PRINTER

COMPUTER	COMMAND
IBM PC, Macintosh, TRS-80	LLIST
Apple II	PR#1 LIST
Commodore 64	OPEN 4,4 CMD 4 LIST

Should you find errors in your program, no matter how minor, you must correct them or the program will not run properly, if indeed it will run at all. In appendix A, we demonstrate how changes can be made in program code after it has been entered into the computer's memory.

Testing and Running a Program

We have now discussed the first three steps of the program development cycle: analyzing the problem, designing a program to solve it, and coding the program. The last step is to test the program.

Testing the program ensures that it is free of errors and that it in fact does solve the given problem. Testing takes place throughout the entire program development cycle; at each step, you should check your work for mistakes. The ultimate test, however, involves executing (or **running**) the program to see if it works correctly.

> To run a program, type the system command RUN and
> press the Enter key.

When we run the program in example 1.9, the following text is displayed on the screen:

```
RUN

THE VALUE OF AN INVESTMENT OF 4500 DOLLARS
INVESTED AT A RATE OF 9.6 PERCENT
COMPOUNDED 4 TIMES PER YEAR
FOR 2 YEARS IS
 5440.169 DOLLARS.
```

The question now arises: Is the program working properly; that is, has it produced a correct result? The computed value seems reasonable but is difficult to check by hand. To test the program, we can use simpler input data by changing statements 270–300 so that, for example, P = 100, R = 0.1, N = 1, and T = 1, and run the program again. This time we can compute the final amount by hand (A = 100(1 + 0.1) = 110) and check this answer against the computer's. If they are the same, it is likely that the result obtained with the original data is correct as well. If they are not the same, we have to *debug* the program.

Debugging a Program

The process of finding and correcting program errors—getting the bugs out—is called **debugging.** The two types of errors that may arise are known as syntax errors and logic errors. A **syntax error** is a violation of BASIC's rules of statement structure. Syntax errors can be caused by misspelling or omitting a keyword or by failing to put the statement in the proper format; some examples are shown in table 1.7.

TABLE 1.7   SOME SYNTAX ERRORS

STATEMENT		ERROR
320	PINT X	PRINT misspelled
500	LET Y + 1 = Y	Only a variable is allowed on the left of the equal sign
650	PRINT HELLO"	Quotation mark missing

Fortunately, most syntax errors will be caught by the computer when the program is run, and an error message (or **diagnostic**) will be displayed. For example, after executing statement 650 in table 1.7, a message similar to the following one will be printed:

```
SYNTAX ERROR IN 650
```

A **logic error** is one that leads to incorrect results when the program is executed, or it may lead to no results at all. It can occur because of faulty analysis, faulty design, or a failure to code the program correctly.

EXAMPLE 1.10   Statement 220 is supposed to copy the value of X into the variable Y.

```
200    LET X = 1
210    LET Y = 2
220    LET X = Y
```

Instead, the value of Y is copied into X.

In the following program segment, the PRINT and LET statements have to be interchanged.

```
100 REM    THIS PROGRAM PRINTS THE NUMBER 5.
110    PRINT X
120    LET X = 5
130    END
```

Unfortunately, most logic errors will not be detected by the computer and it may be difficult for the programmer to find them. The Programming Pointers give tips on preventing, finding, and correcting logic errors.

1.6   PROGRAMMING STYLE

A program will run properly as long as its logic and syntax are correct. This is all that the computer requires. Nevertheless, to be considered good, a program must do more. It must be easy for people to use and easy for programmers to read.

A program is easy to use if its users are not burdened with unnecessary complications of any kind while running it. We say that such programs are **user-friendly.** Remember that the users of a program are rarely familiar with the code itself. If a user needs any information about the program while running it, that information must be displayed on the screen.

The program's code also must be written in such a way that other programmers can understand it easily. A successful program will be modified several times during its lifetime, to add features, reflect changing conditions, or just correct errors. In fact, this process of **maintaining** or **updating** programs accounts for the majority of work done by professional programmers. To make this maintenance work less painful, a program must be easy to read. The original programmers also reap a benefit from the increased readability. Their code is likely to produce fewer errors and those that do occur will be easier to find and correct.

Concepts that make a program easier to read and easier to use are grouped together under the general heading of **programming style.** Some of the elements of programming style have already been demonstrated in this chapter's sample programs; we will describe them in the remainder of this section. Many more style elements will appear throughout the text as Style Pointers.

STYLE POINTER Use Line Numbers of Equal Length
and Increments

One of the ways to make a program more readable is to type its statements in a consistent manner. Line numbers that all contain the same number of digits have a nice visual appeal. Compare the following:

	Poor		**Better**
80	LET A = 12	180	LET A = 12
90	LET B = 14	190	LET B = 14
100	LET C = 16	200	LET C = 16
110	LET D = 18	210	LET D = 18

For short programs (fewer than 80 or 90 lines), we usually use three-digit numbers. For longer programs, four- or five-digit numbers become necessary. It is also common practice to choose line numbers so that each is 10 more than the preceding one.

STYLE POINTER Use Comments

An important way to make your programs more readable is to document them, to provide the reader with commentary on the code in the program itself. This is done by means of REM statements, the contents of which the computer ignores. They are there solely for the benefit of those (humans) reading the program. The contents of REM statements are called comments or **internal documentation.**

STYLE POINTER   Provide Header Comments

The first program lines should be a sequence of REM statements supplying the reader with general information about the program. These are called **header comments.** They should include:

1. The program title (and version number, if more than one).
2. The authors' names (and affiliation—company or class—if appropriate).
3. The date on which the program was completed.
4. A brief description of the program.
5. References to publications that might enlighten the reader.
6. Identification of major program variables.

EXAMPLE 1.11   The following program segment contains appropriate header comments:

```
100 REM    ****    AREA COMPUTATION    ****
110 REM
120 REM    S. VENIT              JANUARY, 1987
130 REM
140 REM    THIS PROGRAM COMPUTES THE AREA OF A REGULAR POLYGON
150 REM    USING THE FORMULA IN "GEOMETRY" BY R. CHIP AND P.
160 REM    DALE (ACME PUBLICATIONS, 1876), P. 1514.
170 REM
180 REM    VARIABLES:
190 REM       N ... NUMBER OF SIDES OF POLYGON
200 REM       L ... LENGTH OF EACH SIDE
210 REM       A ... AREA OF POLYGON
```

STYLE POINTER   Provide Step Comments

You should also use REM statements in your programs to explain upcoming blocks of code. These **step comments** provide an outline of your program for someone reading the code. Remember: Those reading your code are programmers, so you needn't over-explain things.

Since our first programs are relatively short and simple, step comments will be limited to phrases such as "INPUT BLOCK" or "COMPUTATION BLOCK" for a while. As our programs become more complex, our step comments will become more varied and more important.

STYLE POINTER   Use Descriptive Variable Names

Your variable names should remind the reader of the quantities they represent. In BASIC dialects that allow long variable names (see table 1.3 in section 1.2), this is easy to do, but even in a BASIC version that recognizes only the first two characters, we can follow this advice.

VARIABLE	POOR NAME	BETTER NAME	
		Short	Long
Grade on test 1	X	G1	GRADE1
Average score	Y	A	AVG
Price	Z	P	PRICE

STYLE POINTER   Distinguish Comment from Code

Every comment in your program will be preceded by the BASIC keyword REM. Nevertheless, you should type your program so that it is evident from just looking at it what is comment and what is code. You can achieve this by doing two things. First, indent the code statements, but not the REM statements. (This cannot be done on the Apple II and Commodore 64 computers.) Second, separate each block of REM statements from the preceding and following lines of code by a blank line. Unfortunately, many versions of BASIC do not allow a completely blank line. To simulate one, we will use what we call a blank REM: a statement containing only the keyword REM.

Poor

```
200 REM    PROGRAM CONTINUES
210 LET X = 1
220 REM PRINTING BEGINS
230 PRINT "HI"
```

Better

```
200 REM    PROGRAM CONTINUES
210 REM
220    LET X = 1
230 REM
240 REM    PRINTING BEGINS
250 REM
260    PRINT "HI"
```

STYLE POINTER   Identify Your Output

The output produced by your program should stand on its own. It should make sense to someone who has no knowledge whatsoever of the workings of the program that produced it. In particular, never print numbers without an explanation of what they represent. Be liberal with your use of messages to the user.

Poor

```
300 PRINT X; Y; AVG
```

Better

```
300 PRINT "THE AVERAGE OF THE NUMBERS:"
310 PRINT X; "AND "; Y "IS "; AVG
```

REVIEW EXERCISES

Short Answer

For each statement in exercises 1 and 2, identify
    a. the line number   b. the BASIC keyword
    c. the variables   d. the constants

1. `230    LET X = A + B — 1`

2. `350    PRINT 2 * W3 ^ N`

3. a. Identify the valid BASIC constants.
   `21.00   21,000   .0   —7.3   +5.1   $3.21`

   b. Identify the valid BASIC variable names.
   `A1    A@B    1A    X 2    Q`

4. Find the value of each numeric expression.

   a. $2 \wedge 3 - 7 * 3 + 1$

   b. $5 * 3 / 10 - 4 + 7$

   c. $4 * 3 \wedge 2 + 5 / 2 / 2$

5. Assume that the values of A, B, and X are 1, 2, and 17, respectively. What is the value of X after each statement is executed?

   a. `280    LET X = 2 * A ^ 4 — (7 — B) + B / 6 * B`

   b. `320    LET X = A ^ 2 + (—A) ^ 2 * (10 — B)`

   c. `350    LET X = X + 1`

6. Which of the following statements are true? Which are false?

   a. REM statements display information for the program's user.

   b. LET statements can be used to assign values to variables.

   c. Before we code a program, we should design it.

   d. A program with no syntax errors will always run correctly.

   e. Good programming style results in programs that are easier to read and easier to use.

Debugging

7. The following program segment is supposed to find the area of a rectangle with sides L and W, but it contains errors. Find and correct them.

```
200        LET L = 16.3
210        LET W = 21,8
220        LET A = (L + W) / 2
230        PRINT THE AREA IS; A
```

8. Find the syntax errors in the following statements:

```
a. 200      PRINT WE ARE NUMBER ONE!
b. 220      POINT 7 * (X — 7)
c. 240      LET 5 = X3
```

The programs in exercises 9 and 10 contain syntax and logic errors. Find and correct them.

```
9.  100 REM    THIS PROGRAM COMPUTES AND PRINTS THE
    110 REM    AVERAGE OF THREE NUMBERS.
    120        LET A = 14.2, LET B = 121, LET C = 7.
    130        LET X = A + B + C
    140        PRINT "X"
    150        EMD
```

```
10. 100        THIS PROGRAM COMPUTES AND PRINTS
    110        A TEN PERCENT COMMISSION ON GROSS SALES
    120        LET X = $45,231
    130        LET Y = X * R
    140        PRINT THE COMMISSION IS
    150        PRIT X
    160        END
```

Skill Builders

In exercises 11–14, what is the output of each program?

```
11. 100        PRINT "WELCOME TO THIS PROGRAM."
    110        PRINT "IT DOES NOTHING."
    120 REM    WELL, ALMOST NOTHING
    130        END
```

```
12. 100 REM    A SIMPLE PROGRAM
    110        PRINT "HERE IT IS!"
    120        LET A = 15.3
    130        LET B = 5.1
    140        PRINT "THE DIFFERENCE IS"
    150        PRINT A — B
    160        END
```

```
13. 100        LET X = 14
    110        PRINT X
    120        LET X = X — 5
    130        PRINT X; X — 5
    140        LET Y = 3
    150        LET X = Y
    160        PRINT "Y"; Y
    170        END
```

```
14. 100        LET A = 3
    110        LET B = 4
    120        PRINT "THE SUM OF THE SQUARES OF"
    130        PRINT A; "AND "; B;
    140        PRINT "IS "; A ^ 2 + B ^ 2
    150        END
```

PROGRAMMING PROBLEMS

Write a BASIC program to solve each of the following problems. Go through the steps of the program development cycle.

1. At the beginning of a trip, a car's odometer reads 43,276; at the end, 44,871. If 62.3 gallons of gasoline were used on the trip, how many miles per gallon did the car get?

2. The value of Amalgamated Limited stock at the end of 1986 was $13.56 per share. At the beginning of the year it was $11.35 per share. What was the average monthly increase for the stock?

3. Sally Shopwise needs to buy detergent. The 48-ounce box costs $2.25, the giant economy 5-pound box is $4.10. What is the unit price (the cost per ounce) for each of them?

4. Before purchasing her detergent, Sally remembers that she has a 25-cent coupon for the smaller size and a 50-cent coupon for the larger one. Modify the program in problem 3 to find her cost per ounce with the coupons.

5. Moving right along, Sally comes to the peanut butter display. Sticky Brand peanut butter is on sale today for 13.5 percent off. If it regularly costs $2.19 for the jar, what is its cost today?

6. At last Sally makes it to the bank to cash her weekly paycheck. She makes $23.00 per hour as a computer programmer with time-and-a-half for overtime (over 40 hours per week). This week she worked 52 hours. From her gross salary, her company deducted 30 percent for state and local taxes, 5.25 percent for retirement, and $3.00 for parking. What is her net pay (gross pay minus deductions) this week?

7. Bob Hurt took a client to dinner at the Very Plush restaurant and the bill (before tax) came to $423.73. The tax rate was 8.25 percent and Bob decided to leave a 12 percent tip. What was the total damage to Hurt?

8. After his recent dinner fiasco, Bob had to cash in a $2,500.00 certificate of deposit. The certificate was paying 5.35 percent simple interest (Bob wasn't very good at handling money) and had been in the bank for one-and-a-half years. If the early withdrawal penalty is three months' interest, how much money does Bob receive from the bank? (The interest from an investment of P dollars at R percent simple interest held for K months is $I = P*R*K/1200$.)

INPUT AND
OUTPUT

In chapter 1, you saw how the LET and PRINT statements provide simple ways to supply input and display output for BASIC programs. In this chapter, you will learn more powerful means of performing input and output (I/O) operations. This will be accomplished by the use of the INPUT, READ, and PRINT USING statements as well as additional features of the PRINT statement.

2.1   THE INPUT STATEMENT

Using the LET statement to supply input data for a program (as we did in chapter 1) is often less than ideal. For example, consider the compound interest program discussed in section 1.4 (example 1.9). If we wanted to run this program with values other than the given ones for the input variables, we would have to modify the program itself (by changing some LET statements). A better solution to this problem is illustrated in the next example.

EXAMPLE 2.1
```
100 REM    **    BREWSTER'S THOUSANDS — VERSION 2    **
110 REM
120 REM       S. VENIT         FEBRUARY, 1987
130 REM
140 REM  THIS PROGRAM COMPUTES THE VALUE OF AN INVESTMENT
150 REM  USING THE COMPOUND INTEREST FORMULA:
160 REM     A = P * (1 + R / N) ^ (N * T)
170 REM
180 REM  VARIABLES:
```

```
190 REM       P ... INITIAL AMOUNT INVESTED
200 REM       R ... ANNUAL INTEREST RATE (AS A DECIMAL)
210 REM       N ... FREQUENCY OF COMPOUNDING (TIMES PER YEAR)
220 REM       T ... PERIOD OF INVESTMENT (IN YEARS)
230 REM       A ... VALUE OF INVESTMENT AFTER T YEARS
240 REM
250      PRINT "THIS PROGRAM COMPUTES THE FUTURE VALUE"
260      PRINT "         OF AN INVESTMENT"
270 REM
280 REM    INPUT BLOCK
290 REM
300      PRINT "ENTER THE AMOUNT INVESTED"
310      INPUT P
320      PRINT "ENTER THE ANNUAL INTEREST RATE (AS A DECIMAL)"
330      INPUT R
340      PRINT "ENTER THE NUMBER OF TIMES PER YEAR COMPOUNDED"
350      INPUT N
360      PRINT "ENTER THE LENGTH OF THE INVESTMENT (IN YEARS)"
370      INPUT T
380 REM
390 REM    COMPUTATION BLOCK
400 REM
410      LET A = P * (1 + R / N) ^ (N * T)
420 REM
430 REM    OUTPUT BLOCK
440 REM
450      PRINT "THE VALUE OF AN INVESTMENT OF"; P; "DOLLARS"
460      PRINT "INVESTED AT A RATE OF"; R * 100; "PERCENT"
470      PRINT "COMPOUNDED"; N; "TIMES PER YEAR"
480      PRINT "FOR"; T; "YEARS IS"
490      PRINT A; "DOLLARS."
500 REM
510      END
```

Notice that except for lines 250–370, the program in example 2.1 is virtually identical to the one in example 1.9. Statements 250 and 260 display a **welcome message,** some general information about the program, for the user. This message often consists of a very brief description of the program. (Remember: The user is rarely familiar with the code and will not see REM statements 140–160 while running the program.)

When each INPUT statement (lines 310, 330, 350, and 370) in example 2.1 is executed, program execution halts temporarily and a symbol, usually a question mark, is displayed on the screen. This is a signal to the user to enter input data, which is done by typing the appropriate number and pressing the Enter key. The computer then assigns the number entered to the variable appearing in the INPUT statement and resumes execution of the program.

For example, when statement 310 of our program is processed, execution pauses and a ? is displayed. If, for example, the user now types 1000 and presses the Enter key, this value will be assigned to the variable P and execution will continue with statement 320.

Let us follow a typical run through lines 250–370 of the program, showing the text that will appear on the screen when these statements are executed.

```
THIS PROGRAM COMPUTES THE FUTURE VALUE        [the welcome
              OF AN INVESTMENT                   message]
ENTER THE AMOUNT INVESTED                     [statement 300]
? 1000 ◄──────────────────────────────────── typed by user
ENTER THE ANNUAL INTEREST RATE (AS A DECIMAL) [statement 320]
? .10 ◄───────────────────────────────────── typed by user
ENTER THE NUMBER OF TIMES PER YEAR COMPOUNDED [statement 340]
? 4 ◄─────────────────────────────────────── typed by user
ENTER THE LENGTH OF THE INVESTMENT (IN YEARS) [statement 360]
? 7 ◄─────────────────────────────────────── typed by user
```

Notice that each INPUT statement is preceded by a PRINT statement indicating the type of data the user is to enter. These messages are called **input prompts.**

STYLE POINTER   Use a Prompt before Every INPUT

The only information that an INPUT statement (without a prompt) will display on the screen is a question mark. Therefore, a PRINT statement prompting the user for the requested data should precede each INPUT.

Poor		**Better**	
240	INPUT S	240	PRINT "ENTER MILES TRAVELED"
250	INPUT T	250	INPUT S
		260	PRINT "ENTER TIME ELAPSED"
		270	INPUT T

Once the data are entered into our program, the final value of the investment can be computed in line 410 and the result displayed by line 490. (If our previous data—P = 1000, R = .10, N = 4, and T = 7—are used, 1996.494 dollars would be printed as the value of A.) Notice that we also display the values of the input data (lines 450–480). This is called **echo printing** the input.

INPUT with Several Variables

We can use a single INPUT statement to enter several data items. This is done by listing the corresponding variables, separated by commas, after the word INPUT.

EXAMPLE 2.2   Consider the following modification of lines 320–370 of example 2.1:

```
320      PRINT "ENTER THE FOLLOWING, SEPARATED BY COMMAS:"
330      PRINT "   THE ANNUAL INTEREST RATE (AS A DECIMAL)"
340      PRINT "   THE NUMBER OF TIMES PER YEAR COMPOUNDED"
350      PRINT "   THE LENGTH OF THE INVESTMENT (IN YEARS)"
360      INPUT R, N, T
```

Here, statements 320–350 supply the input prompt. When the INPUT statement (line 360) is processed, execution pauses and a ? is displayed. The user now enters the requested data by typing three numbers, separated by commas, and then pressing the Enter key.

For example, suppose the user responds to the ? as follows:

```
?  .10,  4,  7
```

In this case, the first number typed will be assigned to the first variable in the INPUT list (R = .10); the second number, to the second variable (N = 4); and the third number, to the third variable (T = 7). Execution will then continue with the next statement in the program. Thus, the net effect of the new statements 320–360 will be the same as that of statements 320–370 in example 2.1.

Prompt and INPUT Combined

In most versions of BASIC, we need not use two separate statements for printing the prompt and accepting the user's input; both actions can be accomplished with a single INPUT statement. For example, the pair of statements

```
200      PRINT "WHAT IS THE RADIUS OF THE CIRCLE?"
210      INPUT R
```

can be replaced by the single statement

```
300      INPUT "WHAT IS THE RADIUS OF THE CIRCLE"; R
```

When this type of INPUT statement is executed, the text within the quotation marks is printed, immediately followed by a question mark. Execution then pauses for user input, which is displayed on the same line as the prompt, and execution continues after the Enter key is pressed. Hence, if the user types 10 in response to the prompt of statement 300, the following line will be displayed:

```
WHAT IS THE RADIUS OF THE CIRCLE? 10
```

NOTE   On some systems, you can prevent the question mark from appearing after the prompting message by replacing the semicolon with a comma. For example, when the statement

```
300      INPUT "ENTER THE RADIUS OF THE CIRCLE ", R
```

is executed, the following will appear on the screen:

```
ENTER THE RADIUS OF THE CIRCLE
```

```
The INPUT statement

Form      INPUT ["prompt";] variable, variable, . . .
          where the brackets indicate that the prompt is optional

Action    The prompt message, if present, is printed. Then execution
          pauses, a ? is displayed, the data entered are assigned to
          corresponding variables, and execution continues.

Examples  320    INPUT X, Y
          360    INPUT "EMPLOYEE NUMBER"; NUM
```

2.2 CHARACTER STRINGS

In this section you will learn how to use the LET, PRINT, and INPUT statements with *character strings* such as names and addresses.

String Constants and Variables

Any symbol that can be typed at the computer keyboard is called a **character.** For example, all letters and digits are characters as are the symbols for semicolon, period, and the blank, what you get when you press the space bar. (The standard character set used by most computers is given in section 7.4.) A **character string,** or more simply, a **string,** is a sequence of characters. Thus,

```
12AB?5(
JOHN DOE
```

and

```
Z
```

are all strings. Notice that even a single character is a string.

In chapter 1, we discussed numeric constants. Character strings make up another kind of BASIC constant; a **string constant** is a character string enclosed in quotation marks. By means of a LET or INPUT statement, a string constant can be assigned to a variable, which is then called a **string variable.** Its value may be changed as the program is executed.

To represent a string variable, we must use a valid numeric variable name immediately followed by a dollar sign, $.

TABLE 2.1 SOME VALID AND INVALID STRING VARIABLE NAMES

VALID		INVALID	
A$		A1	(No dollar sign)
X1$		$X	(Dollar sign must be last character)
X0$			
GRADE$	(Valid in most versions of BASIC)	A $	(No blanks are allowed)
STU$			

The LET and PRINT statements can be used with string variables in the same way you have been using them with numeric variables.

EXAMPLE 2.3 Consider the code

```
230      LET H$ = "HELLO"
240      LET G$ = "GOODBYE"
250      LET G$ = H$
260      PRINT G$
```

Statements 230 and 240 assign the strings HELLO and GOODBYE to the variables H$ and G$, respectively. Statement 250 then replaces the value of G$ (GOODBYE) with that of H$ (HELLO). Thus, when statement 260 prints the current value of G$, HELLO will appear on the screen.

PROGRAMMING POINTER

In a LET statement, the left and right sides of the equal sign must be of the same type; that is,

1. If there is a numeric variable on the left side, the right side must then be an expression whose value is a number.

2. If there is a string variable on the left side, the right side must then be a string constant or string variable.

INPUT with String Variables

Like the LET and PRINT statements, the INPUT statement handles string variables in the same way it does numeric ones. This is illustrated by the next program.

EXAMPLE 2.4
```
100 REM   ******   STUDENT GRADES   ******
110 REM   S. VENIT              FEBRUARY, 1987
120 REM
130 REM   THIS PROGRAM INPUTS A STUDENT'S TEST SCORES AND
```

```
140 REM     PRINTS OUT HIS OR HER TEST AVERAGE
150 REM
160 REM     VARIABLES:
170 REM        N ........... NUMBER OF TESTS TAKEN
180 REM        STU$ ........ NAME OF STUDENT
190 REM        T1, T2, T3 ... SCORES ON TESTS
200 REM        AVG ......... AVERAGE SCORE
210 REM
220     PRINT "           STUDENT GRADE PROGRAM"
230 REM
240 REM     INPUT BLOCK
250 REM
260     PRINT "ENTER THE STUDENT'S NAME FOLLOWED BY THE NUMBER"
270     PRINT "OF TESTS TAKEN (SEPARATE BY COMMA)"
280     INPUT STU$, N
290     PRINT "ENTER THE SCORES ON THE TESTS"
300     INPUT T1, T2, T3
310 REM
320 REM     COMPUTATION BLOCK
330 REM
340     LET AVG = (T1 + T2 + T3) / N
350 REM
360 REM     OUTPUT BLOCK
370 REM
380     PRINT "STUDENT NAME:    "; STU$
390     PRINT "TEST SCORES:    "; T1; T2; T3
400     PRINT "THIS STUDENT'S AVERAGE IS "; AVG
410 REM
420     END
```

In this example, statement 220 gives the welcome message. This is followed by a prompt (lines 260 and 270) and the first INPUT statement (line 280). As usual, when statement 280 is processed, execution pauses and a ? is displayed on the screen. The user must then type a character string (say, JOHN SMITH), a comma, and a number (say, 3); and then press the Enter key. At this point, JOHN SMITH will be assigned to STU$ and the number 3 to N. (Notice that string and numeric variables may be mixed in an INPUT list as long as the user types the appropriate constant for each.)

Execution now continues with the second prompt and INPUT in lines 290 and 300. Here, three numbers must be typed by the user (say, 82, 75, and 92). These are then assigned to the variables T1, T2, and T3. Statement 340 computes the average of these three numbers (83) and statements 380 and 390 echo print the input data. Finally, the student's average is displayed in line 400.

If the program is run with the input just indicated, it will look like this on the screen.

```
           STUDENT GRADE PROGRAM
ENTER THE STUDENT'S NAME FOLLOWED BY THE NUMBER
OF TESTS TAKEN (SEPARATE BY COMMA)
? JOHN SMITH, 3  ◄─────────────────────────── Typed by user
ENTER THE SCORES ON THE TESTS
? 82, 75, 92  ◄──────────────────────────────── Typed by user
STUDENT NAME:   JOHN SMITH
TEST SCORES:     82   75   92
THIS STUDENT'S AVERAGE IS   83
```

NOTE   Character strings, such as JOHN SMITH, entered in response to an INPUT statement need not be enclosed in quotation marks unless they contain commas or desired leading or trailing blanks. For example, to input SMITH, JOHN you must type it enclosed in quotation marks, as "SMITH, JOHN".

PROGRAMMING POINTER

When the user enters a constant in response to an INPUT statement, its type (numeric or string) must be the same as the variable to which it is assigned. Otherwise, the program may run incorrectly or not at all. On some systems, the user may be prompted to enter the data again.

2.3   THE READ AND DATA STATEMENTS

We have thus far discussed two means of providing input data for programs: the LET and INPUT statements. In this section, we will introduce a third means, the READ and DATA statement combination.

The READ and DATA Combination

The READ and DATA statements work as a team. DATA is a non-executable statement that creates a list of numeric and/or string constants to be used by the program; READ assigns values from this list to specified variables. The general form of the READ and DATA statements follows:

The READ and DATA statements

Form	READ variable, variable, . . .
	DATA variable, variable, . . .
Action	The READ statement assigns the next available items in the program's DATA statements to the listed variables.
| **Example** | ```
200    READ X, STU$, Y
         .
         .
         .
300    DATA 4.3, MASSASOIT, 17
``` |

The next example illustrates the use of these statements.
```

EXAMPLE 2.5   Consider the following program segment:

```
200        READ N$, ID
210        READ RATE, HOURS
220 REM
230        LET PAY = RATE * HOURS
240 REM
250        PRINT "EMPLOYEE:   ";  N$;  "        ID NO.:";  ID
260        PRINT "HOURS WORKED:  ";  HOURS
270        PRINT "HOURLY PAY RATE:  ";  RATE
280        PRINT "GROSS PAY:  ";  PAY
290 REM
300        DATA   J.  ADAMS, 23487, 10.80, 38
```

When the READ statement in line 200 is executed, the first two items in the DATA statement (J. ADAMS and 23487) are assigned to N$ and ID, respectively. The second READ statement (line 210) then assigns the next two items in the DATA list (10.80 and 38) to RATE and HOURS, respectively. The rest of the program segment computes this employee's PAY and prints all the input and computed values. The output looks like

```
EMPLOYEE:   J.  ADAMS      ID NO.:  23487
HOURS WORKED:  38
HOURLY PAY RATE:   10.8
GROSS PAY:   410.4
```

We may use as many DATA statements as we like to supply values for a program's READ statements. Prior to execution, the computer combines the items in all the DATA statements into a single list called the **data block.** The items are positioned in this list according to their order of appearance in the program. (The constants within a given DATA statement are listed from left to right and items in a lower-numbered DATA statement are listed before those in a higher-numbered one.)

As an example, the data block for example 2.5 consists of the items listed in its only DATA statement.

```
J.  ADAMS
23487
10.80
38
```

We get exactly the same data block if we replace statement 300 by either of the following sequences of statements:

```
300        DATA  J.  ADAMS
310        DATA  23487, 10.80, 38
```
or
```
300        DATA  J.  ADAMS
310        DATA  23487
320        DATA  10.80
330        DATA  38
```

Since the same data block is created in all three variations on the code (the original and the two just seen), the program will execute the same way regardless of the version used.

PROGRAMMING POINTER

The DATA statements, when taken together, must contain enough constants to satisfy all the READ statements in the program. If there are not a sufficient number of data items, an "out of data" error message will be displayed. Moreover, the type of data item (numeric or string) must be the same as the variable to which it is assigned. Otherwise, a "type mismatch" error will occur.

As with INPUT statements, it is usually not necessary to enclose the string constants appearing in a DATA statement in quotation marks. They are required only if the string contains a comma or leading or trailing blanks. If, for instance, we want to write the employee's name in example 2.5 as ADAMS, JOHN we would have to change statement 300 to

```
300     DATA  "ADAMS, JOHN", 23487, 10.80, 38
```

Data statements may contain any number of items and may be placed anywhere in the program, as long as they are before END. However, most programmers prefer the arrangement indicated in the next style pointer.

STYLE POINTER   Arrange DATA Statements to Improve Readability

DATA statements are usually placed just before a program's END statement. The collection of DATA statements should be set off from the rest of the program by a blank REM, and perhaps an identifying comment. To increase program readability, we normally list as many items in a given DATA statement as will be input by the corresponding READ statement.

Poor	Better
200 READ X	200 READ X
210 READ Y, Z	210 READ Y, Z
220 DATA 2, 3	220 PRINT X; Y; Z
230 PRINT X; Y; Z	230 REM
240 DATA 4	240 DATA 2
250 END	250 DATA 3, 4
	260 REM
	270 END

The RESTORE Statement

Sometimes we would like to reuse the list of items created by the DATA statements; the RESTORE statement allows us to do this. To understand how RESTORE works, let us return to the data block, the list of constants created prior to execution from the program's DATA statements.

Associated with the data block is a data pointer which indicates the next item to be used by a READ statement. At the start of the program, the pointer "points at" the first item in the data block. When a READ statement is executed, as each value is assigned to a variable, the pointer advances to the next item in the data block.

When the RESTORE statement is executed, the data pointer is reset: it returns to the beginning of the data block. In other words, the READ statements executed after a RESTORE takes place access the data block as if the program were being rerun. This is illustrated in the next example.

EXAMPLE 2.6   Consider the following code:

```
200        READ A, B
210        PRINT A; B
220        RESTORE
230        READ A, B, C
240        PRINT A; B; C
250 REM
260        DATA  5, 7, 9, 11
```

The first READ statement assigns the numbers 5 and 7 to the variables A and B, respectively, and these values are displayed by the PRINT statement in line 210. Then, the RESTORE statement resets the data pointer so that it again points at 5. Hence, the second READ statement (line 230) assigns the numbers 5, 7, and 9 to A, B, and C, respectively. (Any excess data in the data block—in this case, the number 11—are ignored.) Finally, these values are printed by statement 240. Thus, the output of this code is

```
5    7
5    7    9
```

The RESTORE statement

Form   RESTORE

Action   Resets the data pointer to the beginning of the data block.

Example   220   RESTORE

2.4   THE PRINT STATEMENT REVISITED

In the first three sections of this chapter, we have discussed the input of data. Here, we return to the subject of output, extending the basic features of the PRINT statement introduced in chapter 1. These enabled us to produce the desired output, but perhaps not in the most desirable form. In this section, you will learn several ways to make your output more pleasing to the eye. This is important for two reasons:

1. A program's output is the solution to the user's problem, so it should be as clear as possible.

2. A program's output is a major way in which the user judges the program, so it should be as impressive as possible.

The Clear Screen Statement

Most versions of BASIC provide a "clear screen" statement that erases the entire screen and positions the cursor in the upper left corner. Table 2.2 shows the form of this statement in several BASIC dialects. In the programs in this text, we will use the *Microsoft BASIC* statement CLS to clear the screen.

TABLE 2.2   CLEAR SCREEN STATEMENTS IN BASIC

COMPUTER	FORM
Apple II	HOME
Commodore 64	PRINT CHR$(147)
IBM PC, Macintosh, TRS-80	CLS
VAX-11	PRINT CHR$(27); "[H"; CHR$(27); "[OJ"

STYLE POINTER   Begin the Program with the Clear Screen Statement

The first executable statement in your program should clear the screen. The welcome message will then be printed on a blank screen for a visually pleasing effect.

The Blank PRINT

To create a "blank line" in the program code, we have been using a blank REM statement, one that contains only the BASIC keyword REM. To create a blank line in program output, we use a blank PRINT statement.

> **To move the cursor to the beginning of the next line,**
> **use a statement containing only the keyword PRINT.**

STYLE POINTER   Use Blank Lines in Output to Improve Readability

You should use blank PRINT statements in your program to improve the readability of your output. In general, one or two blank lines should be created to separate the welcome message from what follows and to isolate the input and output. Let your eyes be your guide. Put blank lines where they will result in better-looking output.

EXAMPLE 2.7   This short program illustrates the use of the clear screen and blank PRINT statements.

```
100 REM    *******   PRINT SQUARE   *******
110 REM    S. VENIT              FEBRUARY, 1987
120 REM
130 REM    THIS PROGRAM PRINTS THE SQUARE OF THE NUMBER INPUT.
140 REM
150 REM    VARIABLES:
160 REM      X ..... THE NUMBER INPUT
170 REM
180      CLS
190      PRINT "     SQUARE PRINTER"
200      PRINT
210      PRINT
220 REM
230      INPUT "WHAT IS THE NUMBER"; X
240      PRINT
250 REM
260      PRINT "THE SQUARE OF "; X; " IS "; X^2
270 REM
280      END
```

Because of statement 180, the program's output is printed on a clear screen. Since each blank PRINT causes one line to be skipped, the result of a typical run looks like this:

```
     SQUARE PRINTER

WHAT IS THE NUMBER? 5

THE SQUARE OF  5  IS  25
```

The TAB Function

On a typewriter, you can set tab stops to make indenting or creating columns a lot easier. In most versions of BASIC, we can achieve the same effect by using the TAB function within a PRINT statement.

The TAB function

Form	TAB (numeric expression) [in a PRINT list]
Action	Evaluates the expression and moves the cursor to this position on the current line.
Example	`200    PRINT TAB(10); "X:"; TAB(2*I+1); X`

EXAMPLE 2.8   Consider the following code:

```
310      LET A = 23.4
320      PRINT "123456789 123456789 123456789"
330      PRINT TAB(12); "OUTPUT"
340      PRINT "NUMBER"; TAB(10); A; TAB(18);
350      PRINT "TWICE"; TAB(24); 2 * A
```

In this example, statement 320 prints column headings as the first line of output. When statement 330 is executed, TAB(12) causes the cursor to move to the 12th horizontal position (the 12th column) on the screen where OUTPUT is printed. After execution of these two statements, the screen shows

```
123456789 123456789 123456789
          OUTPUT
```

and the cursor moves to the first position on the next line.

Statement 340 then prints NUMBER (beginning in column 1), moves the cursor to column 10 (due to TAB(10)), and prints the value of A. Since A is a positive number, it is printed with a leading blank, so the number is actually printed beginning in column 11. The cursor then moves to column 18 (due to TAB(18)).

Because statement 340 ends in a semicolon, statement 350 continues printing on the same line. The word TWICE is displayed beginning in column 18, the cursor moves to column 24, and the value of 2 times A is printed with a leading blank (since it is positive). Thus, the entire output produced is

```
123456789 123456789 123456789
          OUTPUT
NUMBER    23.4    TWICE   46.8
```

The number within the parentheses following the word TAB is called the **argument** of the TAB function. The argument can be a number, a variable or, in general, a numeric expression.

EXAMPLE 2.9   What output is produced by the following code?

```
560      LET I = 4
570      PRINT "***"
580      PRINT TAB(I); "***"
590      PRINT TAB(2*I-1); "***"
```

Statement 570 prints the three asterisks and moves the cursor to the beginning of the next line. When statement 580 is executed, the cursor moves to column 4 (since this is the current value of the TAB argument) and again three asterisks are printed. In statement 590 the numeric expression 2*I − 1 is evaluated and used as the argument for the TAB function, moving the cursor to position 7. Then, one more time, three asterisks are printed. This gives the output

```
***
   ***
      ***
```

The Comma in a PRINT List

An easier to use, although less powerful, type of tabbing can be obtained by separating the items in a PRINT list by commas instead of by semicolons. (This feature works with all BASIC dialects.) When a comma is encountered in a PRINT list, the cursor moves to the next *preset tab stop*. These preset tabs are set by BASIC and cannot be altered by the programmer. Their positions vary somewhat from computer to computer, but typical settings (those of Microsoft BASIC) are in columns 15, 29, 43, and 57, creating *print fields* that are each 14 spaces wide.

EXAMPLE 2.10   The following code is similar to that of example 2.8, but commas are used instead of TAB functions:

```
310    LET A = 23.4
320    PRINT "123456789 123456789 123456789 123456789 123456789"
330    PRINT " ", "OUTPUT"
340    PRINT "NUMBER", A, "TWICE",
350    PRINT  2 * A
```

As in example 2.8, statement 320 simply prints the column headings. Statement 330 demonstrates a way to skip a preset tab. When it is executed, a blank is printed in column 1 (which will not be visible in the output) and, due to the comma separator, the cursor moves to column 15 (the first preset tab). Then, OUTPUT is printed and the cursor moves to the beginning of the next line.

Statement 340 prints NUMBER (beginning in column 1), moves the cursor to column 15 (due to the first comma) and prints the value of A (after a leading blank, since it is positive). The cursor then moves to column 29 (the next preset tab stop) where TWICE is printed. The last comma in statement 340 moves the cursor to column 43 (the next preset tab) and suppresses the carriage return.

> **If a PRINT statement ends with a comma, the carriage return that normally occurs after it is suppressed.**

Thus, the value of $2 * A$, printed by statement 350, is displayed on the same line as NUMBER, the value of A, and TWICE. The output of this code is

```
123456789 123456789 123456789 123456789 123456789
          OUTPUT
NUMBER    23.4          TWICE         46.8
```

NOTE   Semicolons, commas, and TAB functions can all be used in the same PRINT statement. For example, the statement

```
PRINT "HI"; TAB(4); "HO"; "HO", "BYE"
```

will produce the output

```
HI HOHO        BYE
```

The PRINT statement (in its most general form)

Form   PRINT item @ item @ ... @ item [@]
where the word *item* represents a constant, variable or
expression; the symbol @ represents a *separator*—a
semicolon, comma, or TAB function followed by a
semicolon; and the brackets indicate that the final separator
is optional

Action   Displays the value of the items and positions the cursor
according to the type of separator.

Examples
```
350    PRINT
450    PRINT 3 * X, "AND"; TAB(20); A; TAB(2*I)
```

2.5   THE PRINT USING STATEMENT

The PRINT statement provides quite a bit of control over output; the PRINT USING statement can give you even more. Unfortunately, it is not available in all BASIC dialects and when it is available, it varies slightly from version to version. In this section we will discuss some of the features of the Microsoft BASIC version of the PRINT USING statement.

PRINT USING can help create a professional look to your output. It can easily perform tasks that would be difficult or even impossible for the PRINT statement. These include:

Rounding numbers to any specified decimal place
Aligning the decimal point in a column of numbers
Placing commas every three digits in large numbers
Placing a dollar sign in front of a printed number

Printing Numbers in a Specified Form

Let us begin by taking a look at a simple example of the PRINT USING statement.

```
200    PRINT USING "THE NUMBER IS ####.###"; A
```

The string constant following the word USING is called the *format string*. It consists of text to be printed (THE NUMBER IS) and a *format field* (####.###) containing *format symbols* (# and .). The format symbols specify the form that the number will take when it is displayed. When a statement such as this is executed, each number sign (#) is replaced by a digit (or space) and the period (.) is replaced by a decimal point.

For the statement we've just seen, the value of A will be printed using four places in front of the decimal point and three places after it. If the value of A is 21.32, the output will be

```
THE NUMBER IS    21.320
```

In this line of output, there are three spaces printed between IS and 21.320. The first of these is part of the text "THE NUMBER IS ". The other two are leading blanks, placed there because four places were reserved in front of the decimal point for the value of A, but only two were needed. After the decimal point, three places were reserved but only two needed. Here, however, a trailing zero is inserted in the extra place.

The next example illustrates additional features of the PRINT USING statement.

EXAMPLE 2.11   Suppose that A = 4.375 and B = 6 when the following code is executed:

```
200     LET T$ = "A AND B ARE #.### AND #.##"
210     PRINT USING "A AND B ARE #.### AND #.##"; A; B
220     PRINT USING T$; A; B
230     PRINT USING "A, ROUNDED TO THE NEAREST TENTH: #.#"; A
240     PRINT USING "B, WITHOUT A DECIMAL POINT: ##"; B
250     PRINT USING "THEIR SUM: ##.### AND "; A + B ;
260     PRINT USING "THEIR DIFFERENCE: ##.###"; A — B
```

Let us look at the output produced by the code in this example on a line-by-line basis.

Line 210. In this statement, there are two format fields in the format string. The values of the variables are inserted into the format fields in the order in which they appear. Thus, the output produced by statement 210 is

```
A AND B ARE 4.375 AND 6.00
```

Line 220. Here, we use a (previously defined) string variable for the format string instead of a string constant. The effect is the same. Statements 210 and 220 produce the same output.

Line 230. If there are not enough places reserved after the decimal point to print a given value, it will automatically be rounded to fit the space provided. Thus, the value of A in line 230 is rounded to the nearest tenth.

```
A, ROUNDED TO THE NEAREST TENTH: 4.4
```

Line 240. If the decimal point does not appear in the format field (as in line 240), then it will not appear in the printout and the number will be rounded to the nearest integer, if necessary. Thus, the output of line 240 is

```
B, WITHOUT A DECIMAL POINT:  6
```

Lines 250 and 260. These statements illustrate two additional points. First, numeric expressions (A + B and A − B) can appear (after the semicolon) in PRINT

USING statements. Second, if PRINT USING ends with a semicolon, (as in line 250), the carriage return will be suppressed (just as in the PRINT statement). The output of lines 250 and 260 is

```
THEIR SUM: 10.375 AND THEIR DIFFERENCE: -1.625
```

Notice that only one space precedes −1.625. The minus sign takes up one of the two places reserved before the decimal point.

NOTE   If the number to be printed is larger than the specified field width, it will be preceded by a percent symbol when it is displayed. For example, the statement

```
300      PRINT USING "##.##"; 321.6
```

produces the output

```
%321.60
```

The PRINT USING statement

Form   PRINT USING format string; item; item; ...; item [;]
where the words *format string* represent a string constant or variable;
item is a constant, variable, or expression; and the brackets indicate that
the final semicolon is optional

Action   Prints the text in the format string and replaces its format fields with
values of the expressions; then causes a carriage return unless there is a
terminating semicolon.

Examples   In tables 2.3–2.5

TABLE 2.3   THE FORMAT SYMBOLS # AND .

SYMBOL	DESCRIPTION	EXAMPLE	
#	Reserves one place for a digit	200	PRINT USING "###"; 324.7
			Output: 325
.	Indicates the position of the decimal point	250	PRINT USING "#.###"; 1.23
			Output: 1.230

Printing Monetary Amounts

One of the tasks at which PRINT USING excels is printing financial reports. It allows you to easily display monetary amounts in dollars-and-cents notation, with the number preceded by a dollar sign, containing commas every three digits, and rounded to the nearest penny. Descriptions of the format symbols needed to do this are given in table 2.4.

TABLE 2.4   THE FORMAT SYMBOLS $ AND ,

SYMBOL	DESCRIPTION	EXAMPLE	
$	Prints a dollar sign to the left of the leftmost # position (*fixed $*)	300	`PRINT USING "$####.##"; 21.58` Output: `$ ↑ 21.58` └──── two spaces
$$	Prints a dollar sign to the left of the leftmost digit (*floating $*)	350	`PRINT USING "$$###.##"; 21.58` Output: `↑ $21.58` └──── two spaces
,	Prints commas every three digits to the left of the decimal point	400	`PRINT USING "####,.#"; 5432.77` Output: `5,432.8`

Each occurrence of a format symbol reserves one place in the displayed output.

A column of numbers displayed by PRINT USING has a pleasing appearance and is easy to read. The numbers can be printed using the same number of decimal places and with the decimal points aligned. If commas or dollar signs are desirable, they can easily be included. The next example illustrates how PRINT USING is superior to PRINT in this respect.

EXAMPLE 2.12   The following code produces three columns of figures, the first two written in dollars-and-cents form, the third as ordinary numbers:

```
410    PRINT "  FIXED $      FLOATING $     ORDINARY"
420    PRINT "-----------------------------------------,--------"
430    LET X = 217.125
440    PRINT USING "$#####,.##   "; X;
450    PRINT USING "$$####,.##   "; X;
460    PRINT X
470    PRINT USING "$#####,.##   "; 10 * X;
480    PRINT USING "$$####,.##   "; 10 * X;
490    PRINT 10 * X
500    PRINT USING "$#####,.##   "; 10 * X + X / 10;
510    PRINT USING "$$####,.##   "; 10 * X + X / 10;
520    PRINT 10 * X + X / 10
```

The output produced by this code is

```
     FIXED $         FLOATING $      ORDINARY
 - - - - - - - - - - - - - - - - - - - - - - - - - - - -
 $    217.13          $217.13        217.125
 $  2,171.25        $2,171.25        2171.25
 $  2,192.96        $2,192.96        2192.963
```

Notice how the first two columns of numbers (displayed by PRINT USING) are easier to read and more professional looking than the third column (produced by the PRINT statement).

Printing Character Strings

So far we have used the PRINT USING statement to format only numeric values. PRINT USING also provides string formatting symbols. For example, a format field consisting of two backslash (\) symbols separated by n spaces will print the corresponding string variable (or constant) at the left *(left-justified)* in a space $n + 2$ characters wide.

EXAMPLE 2.13   Consider the code

```
710     LET T$ = "TOM"
720     LET D$ = "DICK"
730     LET B$ = "BARTHOLEMEW"
740     LET S1 = 99
750     LET S2 = 57
760     PRINT USING "\    \:###"; T$; S1
770     PRINT USING "\    \:###"; D$; S2
780     PRINT USING "\  \"; B$
```

In statements 760 and 770, there are three spaces between the \ symbols. Consequently, the values of both T$ and D$ are printed, left-justified, in a space five (3 + 2) characters wide. This means that TOM will be followed by two blanks and DICK by one before the next item (the colon) is printed. In statement 780, there are two blanks between the \ symbols, so BARTHOLEMEW is "truncated" to fit in a space four characters wide. Thus, the output is

```
TOM  : 99
DICK : 57
BART
```

Notice how nicely the output data line up in columns.

TABLE 2.5   THE FORMAT SYMBOL \

SYMBOL	DESCRIPTION
\⌣\ n spaces	Prints the string *left-justified* (beginning at the left) in a space of width $n + 2$ characters.
Example	500 PRINT USING "\\ OR \ \"; "HELLO"; "SHERMAN" Output: HE OR SHE

There are other special format symbols that can be used with the PRINT USING statement. These symbols are listed in your computer manual and are used in the same general way as the ones covered in this section. In the next section, we will see a more comprehensive illustration of how the PRINT USING statement is used in a program.

2.6   FOCUS ON PROBLEM SOLVING

In this section (and future sections with the same title), we will illustrate the chapter material by writing BASIC programs to solve given problems. Using the program development cycle, we will analyze the problem, design a program to solve it, code the program, and test it. All programs will be written using good programming style.

Generating an Employee Earnings Report

EXAMPLE 2.14   The Finest Film Company would like to be able to produce an employee earnings report for its salespersons. Given the name of an employee, base monthly salary, and sales for the month, the report would print that employee's gross and net salary. All salespersons receive a 12 percent commission on sales. Deductions are taken for state tax (5 percent), federal tax (25 percent), and retirement fund (6.5 percent of earnings above $500).

PROBLEM ANALYSIS
   Input variables are
       Employee name: EMPLOYEE$
       Base monthly salary: BASE
       Total monthly sales: SALES
   Output variables are
       Commissions for the month: COMM
       Gross salary for the month: GROSS
       State tax deduction: D1
       Federal tax deduction: D2
       Retirement deduction: D3

Relevant formulas are

Commissions for the month: $COMM = 0.12 * SALES$
Gross salary for the month: $GROSS = BASE + COMM$
State tax deduction: $D1 = 0.05 * GROSS$
Federal tax deduction: $D2 = 0.25 * GROSS$
Retirement deduction: $D3 = 0.065 * (GROSS - 500)$
Net salary for the month $= GROSS - (D1 + D2 + D3)$

PROGRAM DESIGN

A pseudocode outline of this program is as follows:

1. Input employee name, base salary, and sales

2. Compute commission, gross salary, and three deductions

3. Print these values and total deductions and net salary for the month, in the following format:

```
EMPLOYEE:        xxxxxxxxx        SALES:           $xxx,xxx.xx

        INCOME                           DEDUCTIONS
BASE SALARY   : $xx,xxx.xx      STATE TAX    : $xx,xxx.xx
COMMISSIONS   : $xx,xxx.xx      FEDERAL TAX  : $xx,xxx.xx
GROSS SALARY  : $xx,xxx.xx      RETIREMENT   : $xx,xxx.xx
                                TOTAL        : $xx,xxx.xx

        NET SALARY IS $xx,xxx.xx
```

A flowchart for this program is given in figure 2.1.

PROGRAM CODE

```
100 REM    **   EMPLOYEE EARNINGS REPORT   **
110 REM
120 REM    S. VENIT           FEBRUARY, 1987
130 REM
140 REM    THIS PROGRAM COMPUTES THE NET MONTHLY INCOME (SALARY
150 REM    MINUS DEDUCTIONS) OF A SALESPERSON.
160 REM
170 REM    VARIABLES:
180 REM       BASE ........  BASE SALARY
190 REM       COMM ........  COMMISSIONS EARNED
200 REM       D1 .........   STATE TAX
210 REM       D2 .........   FEDERAL TAX
220 REM       D3 .........   RETIREMENT CONTRIBUTION
230 REM       EMPLOYEE$ ...  EMPLOYEE NAME
240 REM       GROSS .......  GROSS SALARY
250 REM       SALES .......  EMPLOYEE SALES
260 REM
270     CLS
280     PRINT TAB(20); "FINEST FILM COMPANY"
290     PRINT TAB(18); "EMPLOYEE EARNINGS REPORT"
300     PRINT
310     PRINT
320 REM
330 REM    INPUT BLOCK
340 REM
350     INPUT "ENTER EMPLOYEE NAME  ", EMPLOYEE$
360     INPUT "ENTER BASE MONTHLY SALARY  ", BASE
370     INPUT "ENTER EMPLOYEE SALES FOR MONTH  ", SALES
```

FIGURE 2.1

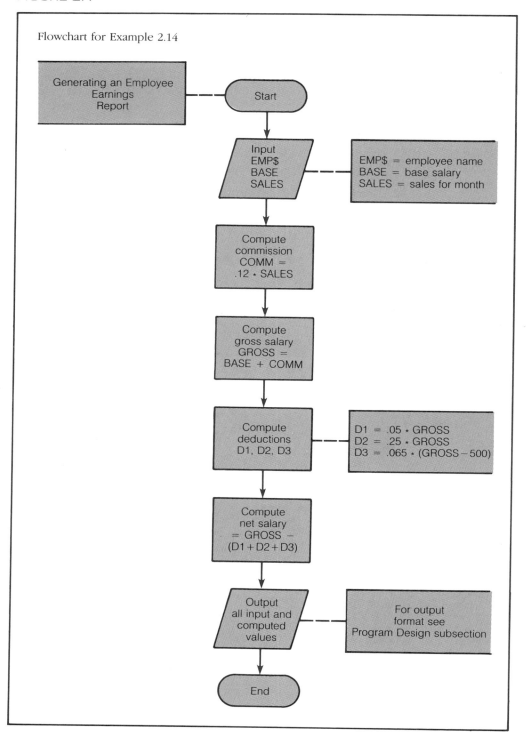

Flowchart for Example 2.14

```
380 REM
390 REM     FOR ALL EMPLOYEES:
400 REM        COMMISSION RATE IS 12%
410 REM          STATE AND FEDERAL WITHHOLDING RATES ARE 25% AND 5%
420 REM          RETIREMENT CONTRIBUTION IS 6.5% ON AMOUNT > $500
430 REM
440      LET COMM = SALES * 0.12
450      LET GROSS = BASE + COMM
460      LET D1 = GROSS * 0.05
470      LET D2 = GROSS * 0.25
480      LET D3 = (GROSS — 500) * 0.065
490 REM
500 REM     OUTPUT BLOCK
510 REM
520      PRINT
530      PRINT
540      LET S$ = "\              \: $#####,.##          "
550      PRINT "EMPLOYEE:", EMPLOYEE$,
560      PRINT USING S$; "   SALES"; SALES
570      PRINT
580      PRINT TAB(10); "INCOME"; TAB(40); "DEDUCTIONS"
590      PRINT USING S$; "BASE SALARY"; BASE; "STATE TAX"; D1
600      PRINT USING S$; "COMMISSIONS"; COMM; "FEDERAL TAX"; D2
610      PRINT USING S$; "GROSS SALARY"; GROSS; "RETIREMENT"; D3
620      PRINT TAB(33);
630      PRINT USING S$; "TOTAL"; D1 + D2 + D3
640      PRINT
650      PRINT TAB(10); "NET SALARY IS ";
660      PRINT USING "$#####,.##"; GROSS — (D1 + D2 + D3)
670 REM
680      END
```

PROGRAM TEST

A run of this program with simple test data shows it to work correctly.

```
                    FINEST FILM COMPANY
                    EMPLOYEE EARNINGS REPORT


ENTER EMPLOYEE NAME  T. JEFFERSON
ENTER BASE MONTHLY SALARY  1000
ENTER EMPLOYEE SALES FOR MONTH  10000


EMPLOYEE:     T. JEFFERSON      SALES      : $10,000.00

     INCOME                         DEDUCTIONS
BASE SALARY  : $ 1,000.00      STATE TAX    : $   110.00
COMMISSIONS  : $ 1,200.00      FEDERAL TAX  : $   550.00
GROSS SALARY : $ 2,200.00      RETIREMENT   : $   110.50
                               TOTAL        : $   770.50

     NET SALARY IS $ 1,429.50
```

REVIEW EXERCISES

Short Answer

1. a. Which of the following are valid string variable names?

    ```
    Q1$    Q    Q $    $Q    Q$    4Q$
    ```

    b. Which of the following are valid string constants?

    ```
    "HELLO"    HELLO    " "    "1"
    ```

2. Determine whether each of the following statements is true or false.
    a. An INPUT statement may contain constants in the input list.
    b. A READ statement allows the user to enter data during program execution.
    c. If a PRINT statement ends with a comma, the carriage return is suppressed.

Debugging

3. Which of the following are valid BASIC statements?

    ```
    a.  200    LET X = Y$        b.  250    LET Q$ = "3"
    c.  300    PRINT X, X$       d.  350    INPUT X, "Y", Z
    ```

4. Correct the syntax errors in the following BASIC statements:

    ```
    a.  200    INPUT X: Y: Z    b.  250    LET X$ = GEORGE
    c.  300    DATA A; B; C      d.  350    PRINT USING "$##": X
    ```

5. The following program segment is supposed to display the values of A and
    B in one column and C and D in another. Correct the errors so that it does.

    ```
    200    READ A, B, C, D
    210    PRINT A, B
    220    PRINT C, D
    230    DATA  3, 5, 7
    ```

6. Why is there a problem using the following program? (Run it, if necessary.)

    ```
    100 REM    **    NAME PRINT    **
    110 REM
    120    PRINT "ENTER NAME"
    130    CLS
    140    INPUT N$
    150    PRINT N$
    160    END
    ```

Skill Builders

In exercises 7–12, what is displayed when each program segment is executed?

```
7.  200    INPUT X                    8.  200    INPUT X1$, X2$
    210    INPUT Y$                       210    PRINT X1$;
    220    PRINT "X:"; X                   220    PRINT X2$
    230    PRINT "Y:"; Y$
```

Input: ? 14.3

Input: ? NO, ON

? JOE

```
9.  200    LET A = 15.7
    210    PRINT "123456789 123456789"
    220    PRINT TAB(12); "GO", "GO"
    240    PRINT TAB(A); A
```

```
10. 200    READ A, B$
    210    PRINT A; B$
    220    RESTORE
    230    READ A, N$, M$
    240    PRINT A; B$; N$; M$
    250    DATA 10.5
    260    DATA JACK, " ,JOE, JIM"
```

```
11. 200    LET X$ = "##.#"
    210    LET V = 21.48
    220    PRINT USING "$####,.##"; 4321.6
    230    PRINT USING X$; 27.483
    240    PRINT USING "V =###.### AND V + 3 =  ##.##"; V; V + 3
```

```
12. 200    LET X$ = "\\"
    210    PRINT USING X$; "OKAY"
    220    PRINT USING X$; X$
    230    PRINT USING "$###.##"; 19.376
    260    PRINT USING "$$##.##"; 19.376
```

13. Write a single PRINT statement containing TABs to produce the following headings centered in the indicated columns:

    NAME (1–14); RANK (15–28); SERIAL NUMBER (29–42)

14. Do exercise 13 without using TABs. (Use the comma separator.)

PROGRAMMING PROBLEMS

Write a BASIC program to solve each of the following problems. Use good programming style and output design in your programs.

1. Input a saleswoman's monthly sales, read her commission rate (as a percentage) from a DATA statement, and print her total commission.

2. Input the list price of an item and the percentage it is being discounted and find the amount of the discount and the sale price.

3. Read a student's name and two test scores from a DATA statement. Print these items and the student's average score.

4. Joe wants to buy a car. He would like to be able to compute the monthly payment (M) on a loan, given the amount of the loan (P), the annual percentage rate of interest (r), and the number of monthly payments (N). The program should allow Joe to input P, r, and N and then compute and print M. Use the formula

$$M = PR(1 + R)^N / ((1 + R)^N - 1)$$

where R = $r/1200$, the monthly interest rate expressed as a decimal.

5. The manager of the Super Supermarket would like to be able to compute the unit price for products sold there. The program should accept as input the name of a product, its price, and its weight in pounds and ounces. It should then determine the unit price (cost per ounce) of the product.

6. The store in problem 5 is now offering 15 percent off on all products. Modify your program to take this into account.

7. The Super Supermarket owners want to compute the gross weekly pay of their employees. Each employee's name, ID number (in six digits), hours worked, overtime hours worked, and pay rate per hour (overtime will be figured as time-and-a-half) are to be input. Output these values and the corresponding gross pay.

8. Modify problem 7 to print an employee's net pay if deductions are taken for taxes (30 percent) and country club fees ($10 per week).

LOOPS

One of the fundamental structures in programming is the **loop,** a series of statements that is executed repeatedly. In this chapter, you will learn to construct loops using IF/GOTO, WHILE/WEND, and FOR/NEXT statements. We will then discuss some of the many ways that loops are used in programming.

3.1 CONTROL STRUCTURES

To increase the readability of your programs, you should write them as a series of properly organized blocks of code called **control structures.** There are three fundamental types:

1. The sequential structure

2. The loop structure

3. The decision structure

A **sequential structure** consists of a series of statements executed in the order given by their line numbers. All the programs you have seen so far have been written as single sequential structures. In the loop and decision structures, at some point a **transfer of control** or **branch** takes place: a statement other than the next higher-numbered one is executed. In the **loop structure,** the result is a series of statements (a block of code) that is executed repeatedly. In the **decision structure,** the branch is used to execute one of several alternative blocks of code and skip the others.

In flowcharts we use a diamond-shaped symbol to indicate a program **branch point,** the point at which a transfer of control may take place. This flowchart symbol is used in figures 3.1 and 3.2 to illustrate typical loop and decision structures. In this chapter we will discuss loop structures; in chapter 4 we will discuss decision structures.

FIGURE 3.1

Flowchart of a Typical Loop Structure

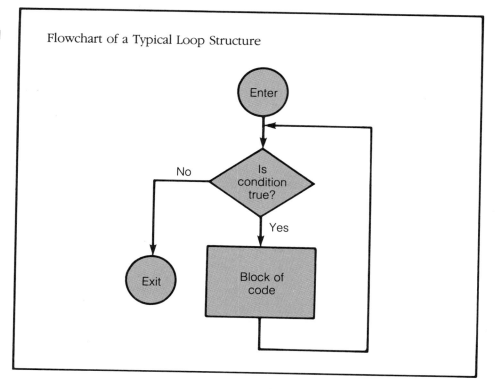

3.2 INTRODUCTION TO LOOPS; RELATIONAL OPERATORS

We begin this section by describing the IF ... THEN and GOTO statements which provide a simple way to implement the *loop structure* of this chapter and the *decision structure* of chapter 4. We then introduce BASIC's *relational operators*, which will also be useful in these chapters.

The GOTO Statement

The GOTO statement is the simplest way to transfer control within a program. When this statement is executed, a branch takes place to the indicated line number. The general form of the GOTO statement follows:

The GOTO statement

Form   GOTO line number

Action   Transfers control to the indicated line number.

Example   9 4 0   G O T O   7 2 0

FIGURE 3.2

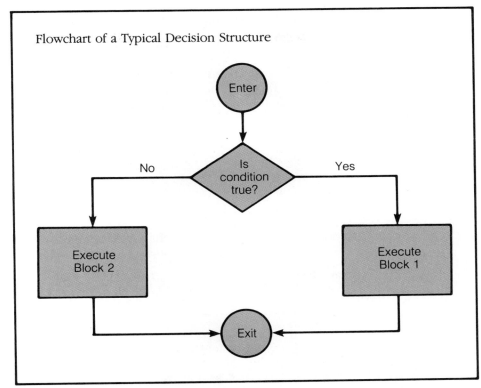

Flowchart of a Typical Decision Structure

EXAMPLE 3.1   This segment of code illustrates how the GOTO statement works.

```
L   ┌  200 REM BEGIN LOOP
O   │  210        PRINT "WE ARE IN THE LOOP"
O   │  220        PRINT
P   └  230    GOTO 200
       240 REM
       250        PRINT "EXECUTION NEVER GETS HERE!"
```

Execution of this segment of code proceeds like this: The message WE ARE IN THE LOOP is displayed and a line is skipped. Then, the GOTO statement (line 230) transfers control to line 200, the number following the keyword GOTO. Once again statements 210 and 220 display the message and skip a line and once again the GOTO transfers control back to line 200.

   Lines 200–230 (the loop) will be executed over and over again, repeating the message WE ARE IN THE LOOP as many times as we like. We say that this block is an *infinite loop*: it would repeat forever if we did not stop it. (On most systems, you can halt program execution in a case like this, or for any reason, by holding down the Control key and pressing either the Break or C key.)

NOTE   In most BASIC dialects, GOTO or GOTO-like statements are needed to implement some control structures. However, improper and/or excessive use of these statements is a major cause of hard-to-read programs. In this chapter and the next, we will demonstrate how to use the GOTO statement properly in those situations when its use cannot be avoided.

The IF ... THEN Statement

The loop in example 3.1 is not a practical one. It repeats forever because there is no statement within it to cause an exit. Whenever we construct a loop, we *must* provide a means for exiting it at the appropriate time. One way of doing this is to use the IF ... THEN statement, which causes a transfer of control if—and only if—its test condition is true. The form of the IF ... THEN statement we will use in this chapter follows:

The IF ... THEN statement (first form)

Form   IF condition THEN line number

Action   Transfers control to the indicated line number if the given condition is true; otherwise, the next statement is executed.

Examples   300   IF A = 19 THEN 210
                400   IF COUNT > LIMIT THEN 360

When an IF ... THEN statement is executed, we say that there is a *conditional* transfer of control; the statement to be executed next depends on whether the test condition is true or false. On the other hand, when a GOTO statement is executed, there is an *unconditional* transfer; execution always moves to the line number following the keyword GOTO.

The IF ... THEN and GOTO statements can be used together to create a loop. This is demonstrated in the next example.

EXAMPLE 3.2   Consider the code:

```
      400        READ N$
      410 REM
L     420        IF N$ = "ZZZ" THEN 460
O     430            PRINT N$
O     440            READ N$
P     450        GOTO 420
      460 REM
      470        DATA   TOM, DICK, HARRY, ZZZ
```

Lines 420–450—the loop—are executed three times, printing (on separate lines) TOM, DICK, and HARRY. After HARRY is read and displayed, the READ statement in line 440 sets N$ equal to "ZZZ". Then, control is transferred (by the GOTO) to the IF ... THEN statement. This time the test condition is true and the loop is exited. A flowchart for this segment of code is given in figure 3.3.

All loops contain control statements (such as IF ... THEN and GOTO) and a block of code to be executed repeatedly. This block of code is called the **body of the loop.** For example, in example 3.2, the body of the loop consists of statements 430 and 440.

FIGURE 3.3

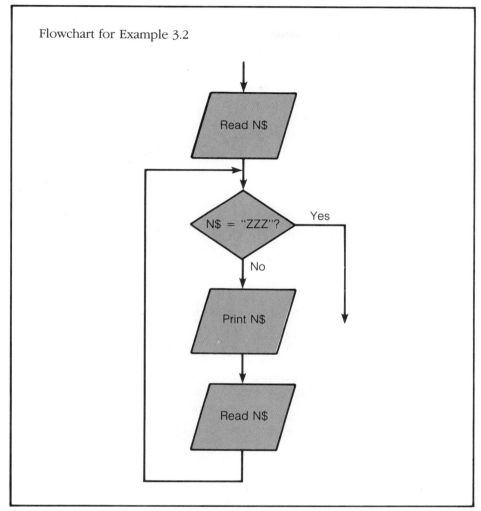

Flowchart for Example 3.2

STYLE POINTER   Indent the Body of a Loop

To improve the readability of your programs, always indent the body of a loop. Indenting makes it easy to see the extent of the loop. Also, for the sake of readability, place blank REM statements before and after the loop.

Poor	Better

```
200     INPUT "N ="; N          300       INPUT "N ="; N
210     IF N < 0 THEN 250        310 REM
220     PRINT N, 2 * N           320     IF N < 0 THEN 360
230     INPUT "N ="; N           330        PRINT N, 2 * N
240     GOTO 210                 340        INPUT "N ="; N
250     PRINT "DONE"             350     GOTO 320
                                 360 REM
                                 370     PRINT "DONE"
```

Relational Operators

In an IF ... THEN statement, the test condition is a **relational expression;** it is either true or false. One way to construct relational expressions is by comparing two constants, variables, or expressions using one of the six **relational operators** listed in table 3.1.

TABLE 3.1   RELATIONAL OPERATORS IN BASIC

OPERATOR	MATH SYMBOL	BASIC SYMBOL
Equal to	$=$	$=$
Not equal to	$\neq$	$<>$
Less than	$<$	$<$
Less than or equal to	$\leq$	$<=$
Greater than	$>$	$>$
Greater than or equal to	$\geq$	$>=$

EXAMPLE 3.3   Let A $=$ -1 and B $=$ 3. In each case, which statement is executed next?

```
a. 200    IF (A ^ 2) >= -B THEN 300
b. 210    IF A <> -1 THEN 310
```

First we must evaluate the condition and determine whether it is true or false.

For a.: Since A ^ 2 $=$ 1, which is greater than or equal to -3 ($-$B), the condition is true and statement 300 is executed.

For b.: A is equal to -1, so the condition is false and statement 220 is executed next.

Character strings can also be compared using relational operators. (See line 420 of example 3.2.) In particular:

A$ = B$ if these strings have exactly the same characters (including blanks) in exactly the same order; if they do not, A$ < > B$.

In section 7.4, we will discuss how strings compare using the other relational operators.

EXAMPLE 3.4   Let X$ $=$ "ANNE" and Y$ $=$ "ANN". Then:

```
a. X$ <> Y$ is true.
b. Y$ = "ANN " is false.
```
⤷space

3.3   TYPES OF LOOPS

In section 3.2 we presented simple examples of loops created by using IF ... THEN and GOTO statements. Here, we will describe several types of loops, classifying them by their *structure* rather than by the statements that make them up. We will also show how the WHILE and WEND statements can be used to construct loops.

Do While and Do Until Loops

With the exception of infinite loops, all loops have an **exit condition**—a test to determine if the loop is to be exited or reentered—within them. The exit condition is normally placed at the beginning or the end of the loop.

EXAMPLE 3.5   Consider the following loops:

```
          Loop A                           Loop B

200 REM                        300  INPUT X$
210          INPUT N           310  IF X$ = "Z" THEN 350
220          PRINT N           320       PRINT X$
230    IF N <> 0 THEN 200      330       INPUT X$
240       ......               340  GOTO 310
                               350  ......
```

The exit condition for Loop A is 'N < > 0' (line 230). When this condition is false (when N = 0), the loop is exited. For Loop B, the exit condition is 'X$ = "Z"' (line 310). Here, exit takes place if the condition is true.

In example 3.5, the exit condition for Loop B is at the top of the loop. The test is made before the loop body is executed and this block of code is executed only while the condition is false. Consequently, Loop B is called a **pretest** or **Do While loop.** For Loop A, the exit condition appears at the bottom, after the body has been executed. This loop continues to be executed until the test condition is false. It is called a **posttest** or **Do Until loop.** The flowcharts and pseudocode for each type of loop are shown in figures 3.4 and 3.5.

Do Until loops can be implemented in BASIC by placing an IF ... THEN statement at the bottom of the loop that causes a branch to the top of the loop if its test condition is true. (See Loop A in example 3.5.) Do While loops can be implemented by using an IF ... THEN statement at the top of the loop and a GOTO statement at the bottom. The GOTO statement transfers control back to the IF ... THEN and the latter causes a branch to the statement after the GOTO if its test condition is true. (See Loop B in example 3.5.)

The crucial difference between a Do While and a Do Until loop is that the body of the former may possibly never be executed, but the body of the latter must be executed at least once. Since it is usually a good idea to test a loop's exit condition before executing the statements within it, Do While loops occur more commonly in programs than Do Until loops. However, Do Until loops are appropriate at times. We will use the example of *data validation* to illustrate this point.

FIGURE 3.4

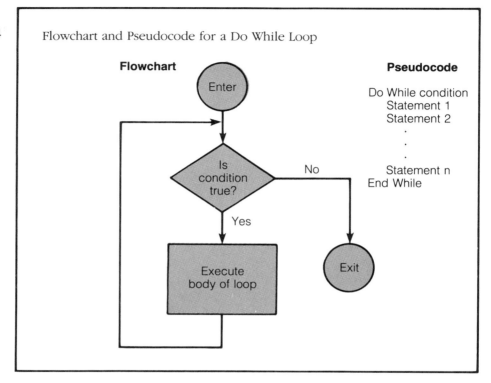

Flowchart and Pseudocode for a Do While Loop

Flowchart

Enter

Is condition true?

No

Yes

Execute body of loop

Exit

Pseudocode

Do While condition
    Statement 1
    Statement 2
    .
    .
    .
    Statement n
End While

Data Validation

Suppose we want the user to enter a positive number at some point during program execution. Then we must place code similar to the following at the appropriate place in the program:

```
xxx    INPUT "ENTER A POSITIVE NUMBER.", N
```

However, despite the input prompt, the user might enter a negative number or zero. To ensure that the program executes properly, we should include code that checks, or **validates,** the input number and requests that the user reenter it if it is not in the proper range. The simplest way to do this is illustrated in the next example.

EXAMPLE 3.6

Validation of input data by a Do Until loop.

```
500 REM      INPUT BLOCK
510 REM
520 REM    REPEAT UNTIL NUMBER ENTERED IS POSITIVE
530             PRINT "ENTER A POSITIVE NUMBER."
540             INPUT N
550        IF N <= 0 THEN 520
560 REM
```

In this form of data validation, we check to see if the input number is in the proper

FIGURE 3.5

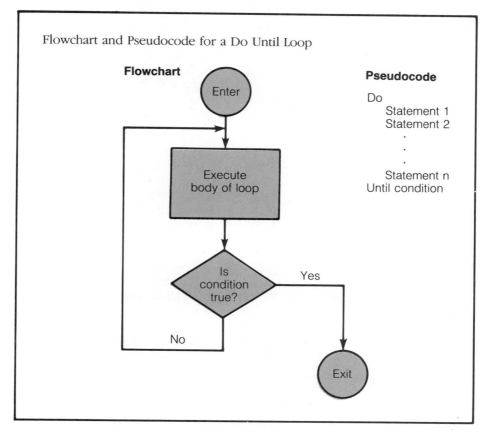

Flowchart and Pseudocode for a Do Until Loop

Flowchart

Enter

Execute
body of loop

Is
condition
true?

Yes

No

Exit

Pseudocode

Do
    Statement 1
    Statement 2
    .
    .
    .
    Statement n
Until condition

range. If it is not, we loop back to the prompt and require that the number be reentered.

Sometimes we may want to emphasize the fact that the user has made an error in entering data by printing a message to this effect. In such a case, we use a Do While loop, as in the next example.

EXAMPLE 3.7   Validation of input data by a Do While loop.

```
600 REM    INPUT BLOCK
610 REM
620     PRINT "ENTER A POSITIVE NUMBER."
630     INPUT N
640 REM
650     IF N > 0 THEN 710
660         PRINT
670         PRINT "THE NUMBER ENTERED MUST BE POSITIVE!"
680         PRINT "         PLEASE TRY AGAIN."
690         INPUT N
700     GOTO 650
710 REM
```

Notice that setting up the loop this way is a little more complicated than the loop in example 3.6 and requires a second INPUT statement (line 690). However, this method of data validation gives us more flexibility. In place of statements 670 and 680, we could provide any useful message or other help for the user. On most microcomputers, we could even issue a warning beep from the speaker.

Data validation is an example of **defensive programming,** writing code that checks during execution for potential errors due to improper data. We will demonstrate other defensive programming techniques in later chapters.

STYLE POINTER   Validate Input Data

Your program should, whenever possible, *validate* input data; that is, check it to determine if it is in the proper range. You can use either Do Until or Do While loops for this purpose as illustrated in examples 3-6 and 3.7.

The WHILE and WEND Statements

Although Do While loops can be implemented by IF ... THEN and GOTO statements, many versions of BASIC provide a much better way. The WHILE and WEND statements of Microsoft BASIC for the IBM PC, Macintosh, and TRS-80 computers do just this. The general form of these statements follows:

The WHILE and WEND statements

Form   WHILE condition
            WEND

Action   The block of code between the WHILE and WEND
            statements is executed repeatedly as long as the given
            condition is true. If the condition is false, the statement
            following WEND is executed.

Example
```
200     WHILE NUM >= 0
210         INPUT NUM
220         PRINT NUM
230     WEND
```

EXAMPLE 3.8   The following program segment performs the same data validation function as the one in example 3.7. This one uses a WHILE/WEND combination to create the loop instead of the IF/GOTO of the previous example. Notice that the test condition in the WHILE statement (N < = 0) is the opposite of the one in the corresponding IF ... THEN statement (IF N > 0 THEN 710) shown in brackets.

```
600 REM     INPUT BLOCK
610 REM
620     PRINT "ENTER A POSITIVE NUMBER."
630     INPUT N
```

```
640 REM
650      WHILE N <= 0           [IF N > 0 THEN 710]
660          PRINT
670          PRINT "THE NUMBER ENTERED MUST BE POSITIVE!"
680          PRINT "         PLEASE TRY AGAIN."
690          INPUT N
700      WEND                    [GOTO 650]
710 REM
```

In example 3.8, we inserted a bracketed segment of code from example 3.7 to contrast the two loops illustrated. In some of the program segments to follow, we will use this system of bracketed code to show the proper alternative for those dialects that must use IF ... THEN and GOTO to implement Do While loops.

NOTE   The WHILE and WEND statements are not available on the Apple II and Commodore 64 computers. On the VAX-11 computer, the keyword NEXT must be used in place of WEND.

STYLE POINTER   Use WHILE and WEND If They Are Available

If your version of BASIC contains the WHILE/WEND combination, use it to construct Do While-type loops. It is easier to read programs that contain WHILE/WENDs than it is to read those with IF/GOTOs. This advice reflects the fundamental rule: avoid the use of GOTO whenever possible.

<table>
<tr><td colspan="2">**Poor**</td><td colspan="2">**Better**</td></tr>
<tr><td>200</td><td>READ X</td><td>300</td><td>READ X</td></tr>
<tr><td>210 REM</td><td></td><td>310 REM</td><td></td></tr>
<tr><td>220</td><td>IF X = 0 THEN 260</td><td>320</td><td>WHILE X <> 0</td></tr>
<tr><td>230</td><td>PRINT X</td><td>330</td><td>PRINT X</td></tr>
<tr><td>240</td><td>READ X</td><td>340</td><td>READ X</td></tr>
<tr><td>250</td><td>GOTO 220</td><td>350</td><td>WEND</td></tr>
<tr><td>260 REM</td><td></td><td>360 REM</td><td></td></tr>
<tr><td>270</td><td>DATA 9, 5, 31, 0</td><td>370</td><td>DATA 9, 5, 31, 0</td></tr>
</table>

3.4   FOR/NEXT LOOPS

In the two previous sections, we constructed loops using the IF/GOTO and the WHILE/WEND statement combinations. In this section, you will learn to create loops with the FOR and NEXT statements.

A type of loop that occurs frequently in programming is one that is *counter-controlled*. A **counter-controlled loop** contains a variable, the **counter,** that keeps track of the number of loop iterations, or passes. The loop is exited when the counter exceeds a preset value.

For example, the following program segment prints the squares of the integers from 1 to N with the aid of a counter-controlled loop. Notice that the counter must be given a starting value (it must be *initialized*), and is increased in value (or *incremented*) on every pass through the loop.

```
440       LET K = 1
450 REM
460       WHILE K <= N
470          PRINT K, K ^ 2
480          LET K = K + 1
490       WEND
500 REM
```

The FOR and NEXT statements provide an easy way to set up a counter-controlled loop. All of the housekeeping chores (initializing the counter, testing for exit, and incrementing the counter) are done automatically by these statements. Using FOR and NEXT statements, the previous program segment can be written as follows:

```
640 REM
650       FOR K = 1 TO N STEP 1
660          PRINT K, K ^ 2
670       NEXT K
680 REM
```

These two segments of code execute in the same way and produce the same results. The FOR and NEXT statements provide for the initialization of K to 1 before the loop is entered, the test to see if K exceeds N, and the increment of K within the loop.

A flowchart describing the action of a FOR/NEXT loop is given in figure 3.6. The general form for the FOR and NEXT statements follows.

The FOR and NEXT statements

Form   FOR var = initial TO limit STEP increment
NEXT var
where var is a numeric variable; and initial, limit, and increment are numeric constants, variables, or expressions

Action   Executes the code lying between the FOR and NEXT statements a fixed number of times (see figure 3.6)

Example   200   FOR COUNT = 5 TO M + 1 STEP I
.
.
.

```
body of loop
```

280   NEXT COUNT

FIGURE 3.6 | The Action of a FOR/NEXT Loop

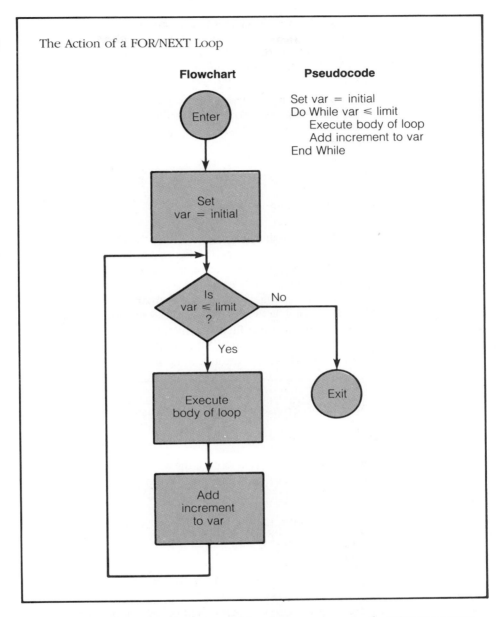

The following terminology is used for the components of a FOR statement.

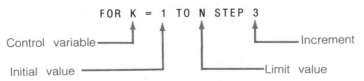

The **control variable, initial value, limit value,** and **increment** taken together are called the **loop parameters.**

NOTES

1. Every FOR statement must eventually be followed by a corresponding NEXT. The variable after the keyword NEXT must be the same as the loop control variable. (In some versions of BASIC, the variable following NEXT may be omitted, but it is better programming practice to include it.)

2. If the loop increment is equal to one, STEP 1 may be omitted from the FOR statement. For example, the statement

```
350     FOR I = M TO N STEP 1
```

has exactly the same effect as

```
350     FOR I = M TO N
```

3. In virtually all forms of BASIC, the FOR/NEXT loop is of the pretest Do While type as indicated in figure 3.6. The major exception is Applesoft BASIC on the Apple II computer. In this version, the exit test takes place after the loop body is executed.

4. In keeping with the Style Pointer of section 3.2, you should indent the body of a FOR/NEXT loop, the statements between FOR and NEXT. You should also use REM statements before and after the loop.

5. In describing FOR/NEXT loops, we will use the flowchart symbol or the pseudocode indicated in figure 3.7.

We will now present examples that illustrate various features of the FOR/NEXT loop.

EXAMPLE 3.9

When a FOR/NEXT loop is exited, the value of the control variable is equal to its value on the last pass plus the value of the increment.

```
200 REM
210     FOR K = 1 TO 5
220         PRINT K;
230     NEXT K
240 REM
250     PRINT
260     PRINT "OUT OF LOOP "; K
```

Five passes are made through this FOR/NEXT loop—one for each value of K as K varies from 1 to 5. On the fifth pass, the number 5 is printed and K is incremented to 6. Since this value exceeds the limit value, the loop is exited and the current value of K (6) is displayed. Thus, the output produced by this code is

```
    1   2   3   4   5
OUT OF LOOP   6
```

If the values of the initial value and the increment are both 1, then the number of loop iterations will be equal to the limit value (as is the case in example 3.9).

FIGURE 3.7

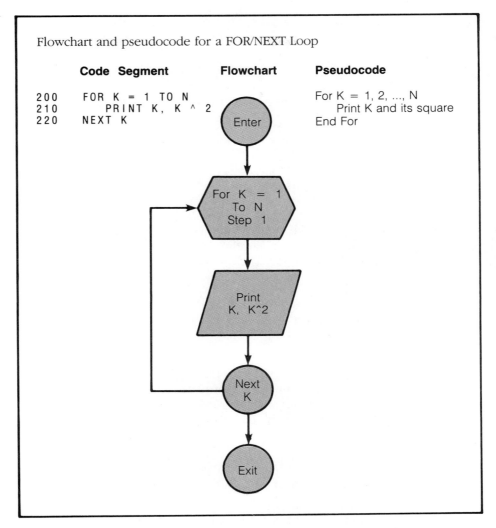

Flowchart and pseudocode for a FOR/NEXT Loop

| **Code Segment** | **Flowchart** | **Pseudocode** |

```
200    FOR K = 1 TO N
210        PRINT K, K ^ 2
220    NEXT K
```

```
For K = 1, 2, ..., N
    Print K and its square
End For
```

However, this is not true when a FOR/NEXT loop has an increment other than 1 as in example 3.10.

EXAMPLE 3.10

This program segment displays the odd numbers between 1 and 30.

```
200 REM
210      FOR N = 1 TO 30 STEP 2
220          PRINT N;
230        NEXT N
240 REM
```

On the first pass through this loop, N is initialized to 1, printed, and incremented by 2 (due to STEP 2 in the FOR statement). Thus, on the second pass, 3 is printed and N is incremented by 2 again. This continues until the 15th pass. On this loop iteration, the value of N (29) is printed and incremented to 31. Since N now exceeds the limit value (30), the loop is exited. The output of this segment of code is

```
1   3   5   7   9   11   13   15   17   19   21   23   25   27   29
```

EXAMPLE 3.11   Numeric expressions may be used for the initial, limit, or increment values.

```
200        LET N = 2
210        PRINT "123456789"
220 REM
230        FOR K = N + 1 TO N ^ 2
240            PRINT TAB(K+1) "***"
250        NEXT K
260 REM
```

Since N = 2, the numeric expressions N + 1 and N ^ 2 in the FOR statement have values 3 and 4, respectively. Hence, the loop is executed twice, first with K = 3 and then with K = 4. Thus, in the first pass, the three asterisks are printed after a TAB(4); in the second one, they are printed after a TAB(5). The output produced by this code is

```
123456789
 ***
 ***
```

EXAMPLE 3.12   By using a negative value for the loop increment, we can step backwards through the loop; that is, cause the control variable to decrease in value with each iteration. For a negative increment, the loop is exited when the value of the control variable becomes less than the limit value.

```
200 REM
210        FOR N = 9 TO 5 STEP −2
220            PRINT N;
230        NEXT N
240 REM
250        PRINT
260        PRINT "ON LOOP EXIT, N = "; N
```

In the first pass through this loop, N is initialized to 9, this value is printed, and then −2 (the increment) is added to it. The value of N is now 7. On the second pass, 7 is printed, and N is incremented (actually, *decremented*) to 5. Finally, on the third pass, 5 is printed, and N is set equal to 3. Since 3 is less than the limit value (5), the loop is exited. Hence, the output of this code is

```
9   7   5
ON LOOP EXIT, N =   3
```

EXAMPLE 3.13   If the loop increment is positive and the initial value is greater than the limit value, the entire FOR/NEXT loop will be skipped.

```
200        PRINT "BEFORE LOOP"
210        LET LIMIT = 4
220 REM
```

```
230        FOR K = 5 TO LIMIT
240           PRINT "HELP, I'M A PRISONER IN A FOR/NEXT LOOP!"
250        NEXT K
260 REM
270        PRINT "AFTER LOOP"
```

Since the initial value (5) is greater than the limit value (4) and the increment is positive (it is 1), this FOR/NEXT loop is skipped. The output of this code is

```
BEFORE LOOP
AFTER LOOP
```

A FOR/NEXT loop will also be skipped if the increment is negative and the initial value is less than the limit value.

3.5   COMPUTING SUMS

When we use a calculator to add a list of numbers, we add each successive number to the *running total*, the sum obtained so far. In effect, we are *looping*: repeatedly applying the addition operation until all the numbers have been added. To write the BASIC code to sum a set of numbers, we do essentially the same thing.

EXAMPLE 3.14   This program illustrates the summing process.

```
100 REM     ***    SUM OF INTEGERS    ***
110 REM
120 REM   S. VENIT          MARCH, 1987
130 REM
140 REM     THIS PROGRAM COMPUTES THE SUM OF THE FIRST N
150 REM     POSITIVE INTEGERS   (N IS INPUT BY THE USER)
160 REM
170 REM     VARIABLES:
180 REM        N ... NUMBER OF INTEGERS IN THE SUM
190 REM        S ... RUNNING TOTAL (ACCUMULATOR)
200 REM
210       CLS
220       PRINT "            INTEGER SUM"
230       PRINT
240 REM
250 REM   INPUT BLOCK
260 REM REPEAT UNTIL ENTERED NUMBER IS POSITIVE
270          PRINT "ENTER A POSITIVE NUMBER.  THE SUM OF THE"
280          PRINT "INTEGERS UP TO THIS NUMBER WILL BE COMPUTED."
290          INPUT N
300          PRINT
310       IF N <= 0 THEN 260
320 REM
330 REM     INITIALIZE ACCUMULATOR
340 REM
350       LET S = 0
360 REM
370 REM     COMPUTE SUM
380 REM
```

```
390       FOR I = 1 TO N
400           LET S = S + I
410       NEXT I
420 REM
430 REM    PRINT SUM
440 REM
450       PRINT
460       PRINT "THE SUM OF THE FIRST"; N;
470       PRINT "POSITIVE INTEGERS IS"; S
480 REM
490       END
```

In order to compute a sum, we use a counter-controlled loop in which the counter keeps track of the number of items that have been added. In this program, the counter is I, the control variable of the FOR/NEXT loop. We also need an **accumulator,** a variable that holds the running total, or the current value of the sum. The accumulator here is the variable S.

To find the sum, we go through the following steps:

1. Input the number, N, of integers to be added (line 290).

2. Set the accumulator, S, equal to zero (line 350).

3. Let the counter run from 1 to N, adding each number to S (lines 390–410).

When we exit the loop, S will have the value 1 + 2 + ... + N, as desired. (See table 3.2 to follow the accumulation of the sum.) Notice that the sum is printed *after* we exit the loop since we want the final total, not the running sum.

A typical run of this program looks like this:

```
                    INTEGER SUM

ENTER A POSITIVE NUMBER.  THE SUM OF THE
INTEGERS UP TO THIS NUMBER WILL BE COMPUTED.
? 4


THE SUM OF THE FIRST 4 POSITIVE INTEGERS IS 10
```

TABLE 3.2   TRACE TABLE FOR EXAMPLE 3.14

		STATEMENT	N	S	I	
	290	INPUT N	4	—	—	
	340	LET S = 0	4	0	—	
First	390	FOR I = 1 TO N	4	0	1	
pass ⟶	400	LET S = S + I	4	1	1	
		390	4	1	2	
Second pass ⟶	400		4	3	2	
		390	4	3	3	
Third pass ⟶	400		4	6	3	
		390	4	6	4	
Fourth pass ⟶	400		4	10	4	
		390	4	10	5	⟶ Exit loop

Using Sentinel Values

The amount of data input to a program often varies from run to run. For example, the number of items analyzed by a statistics program or the number of employees processed by a payroll program would certainly be different for each run. In such cases, the computer needs to know when all the data have been input. This can be handled by placing an additional item, a **sentinel value,** at the end of the data list to act as a signal to the computer that input is complete. The sentinel item, or **end-of-file marker,** must be one that cannot possibly be actual data. For example, if a list of positive numbers is input, the sentinel could be 0; if a list of names is input, the sentinel could be ZZZ.

EXAMPLE 3.15   To find the average (or *mean*) of a set of numbers, we compute their sum and divide by the number of items. This program segment illustrates the use of a sentinel in finding the average of a set of positive numbers.

```
140 REM      INITIALIZE COUNTER AND ACCUMULATOR
150 REM
160      LET COUNT = 0
170      LET SUM = 0
180 REM
190 REM      INPUT NUMBERS AND CALCULATE SUM
200 REM
210      PRINT "ENTER POSITIVE NUMBERS TO BE ADDED."
220      PRINT "        WHEN DONE, ENTER 0."
230      INPUT N
240      WHILE N > 0                        [IF N <= 0 THEN 290]
250         LET COUNT = COUNT + 1
260         LET SUM = SUM + N
270         INPUT N
280      WEND                               [GOTO 240]
290 REM
300 REM      CALCULATE AVERAGE
310 REM
320      LET AVG = SUM / COUNT
```

This program inputs the numbers to be averaged in a loop (lines 240–280) which is exited when the sentinel value (0) is input. Such a loop is sometimes called an **end-of-file loop** (or **EOF loop**). We cannot use FOR and NEXT to create such a loop because we do not know in advance how many loop iterations will be needed. We use instead a WHILE/WEND (or, as we've shown in brackets, an IF/GOTO) construction.

The numbers are input and summed by our EOF loop in a manner similar to that used in example 3.14. However, since we are not using a FOR/NEXT loop here, we must initialize (line 160) and increment (line 250) the counter, COUNT.

After the user has entered all the data, he or she enters the sentinel value, 0, and the loop is exited. The accumulator, SUM, now contains the sum of all the numbers and the value of the counter, COUNT, is how many there are. The average is then computed in statement 320 by simply dividing the sum by the number of items.

3.6 NESTED LOOPS

Programs sometimes use a loop that lies entirely within another one. In such a case, we say that the loops are **nested.** The larger loop is called the **outer loop;** the one lying within it is called the **inner loop.**

EXAMPLE 3.16 The following code contains nested FOR/NEXT loops:

```
         200   FOR I = 1 TO 2
 O   I   210      FOR J = 1 TO 3
 u   n   220         PRINT "OUTER LOOP ITERATION"; I; ";   ";
 t   n   230         PRINT "INNER LOOP ITERATION"; J
 e   e   240      NEXT J
 r   r   250      PRINT
         260   NEXT I
         270   ......
```

When this code is executed, I is set equal to 1 by the FOR I statement and control passes to the FOR J statement, the top of the inner loop. The inner loop is then executed with J = 1 and the NEXT J statement is encountered. This causes control to return to the top of the inner loop (line 210). In this way, the inner loop is executed for all values of its control variable (J = 1, 2, 3) while I remains equal to 1.

After the J = 3 iteration, the inner loop is exited, a blank PRINT takes place (line 250), and control returns to the top of the outer loop. Then I is incremented to 2 and the process is repeated; the inner loop is executed with J = 1, 2, and 3.

The output produced by this code further demonstrates the order in which execution occurs:

```
OUTER LOOP ITERATION 1 ;   INNER LOOP ITERATION 1
OUTER LOOP ITERATION 1 ;   INNER LOOP ITERATION 2
OUTER LOOP ITERATION 1 ;   INNER LOOP ITERATION 3

OUTER LOOP ITERATION 2 ;   INNER LOOP ITERATION 1
OUTER LOOP ITERATION 2 ;   INNER LOOP ITERATION 2
OUTER LOOP ITERATION 2 ;   INNER LOOP ITERATION 3
```

PROGRAMMING POINTER

If two FOR/NEXT loops overlap (have any statements in common), then one loop must be entirely contained within the other; they must be nested. For example:

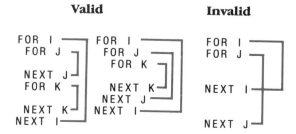

A common error that leads to an invalid overlapping of loops occurs when the NEXT statements are accidentally interchanged, as in

```
620      FOR A = . . . . . . .
630          FOR B = . . . . . . .
                 .
                 .
                 .
780          NEXT A ←————————————————— Should be NEXT B
790      NEXT B ←————————————————— Should be NEXT A
```

If one FOR/NEXT loop is nested within another, BASIC requires that the two control variables be different. However, the loop parameters (the initial, limit, and increment values) of the inner loop can involve the control variable of the outer loop. This feature of nested loops is often useful. It is illustrated in the next example.

EXAMPLE 3.17   Consider the following code:

```
400          FOR I = 1 TO 5
410 REM
420              FOR J = 1 TO I
430                  PRINT "* ";
440              NEXT J
450 REM
460              PRINT TAB(15);
470 REM
480              FOR K = I TO 5
490                  PRINT "? ";
500              NEXT K
510 REM
520              PRINT
530          NEXT I
```

There are two inner loops here: a J loop and a K loop. Let's examine, or *walk through,* a couple of iterations of the outer loop.

With I = 1, the J loop goes through one iteration (J runs from 1 to 1) and so only prints a single asterisk. We then tab over to column 15 and enter the K loop. It goes through five iterations (K runs from 1 to 5) and prints five question marks. Then statement 520 advances the cursor to the next line and I is incremented by 1.

The second time through the outer loop, J runs from 1 to 2, printing two asterisks and K runs from 2 to 5 printing four question marks. In this manner, two triangular patterns are created.

```
*              ? ? ? ? ?
* *            ? ? ? ?
* * *          ? ? ?
* * * *        ? ?
* * * * *      ?
```

3.7   FOCUS ON PROBLEM SOLVING

In this section, we will discuss an application of loops. The program, which performs compound interest calculations, contains both FOR/NEXT and Do Until loops.

The Effects of Compounding

EXAMPLE 3.18

J.R. Allknowing teaches a business class at Podunk University. He would like to demonstrate to his class the effect of compounding interest on the ultimate value of an investment. To do this, he wants to use a computer program to find the value of a $100 investment after ten years, when the interest is compounded at various rates. The interest rate should be input by the user. The user should also be given the option of repeating the computations with another interest rate.

PROBLEM ANALYSIS

The input variable is

Rate of interest in percent: S

The output variable is

Worth of the investment after ten years: A

To compute the value of the investment, we use the compound interest formula with the principal equal to $100 and the term equal to ten years. We use the formula

$$A = 100(1 + R/N)^{10N}$$

where

R is the interest rate as a decimal (determined by S/100); and
N is the number of times per year compounding takes place.

We take R and N to be program variables.

PROGRAM DESIGN

An outline of the program in pseudocode follows. A flowchart is given in figure 3.8.

1. Welcome user

2. Perform calculations

Do
    Input S
    For several values of N
        Compute and print A
    End For
Until user wants to quit

As we add more detail into step 2, we have

FIGURE 3.8

Flowchart for Example 3.18

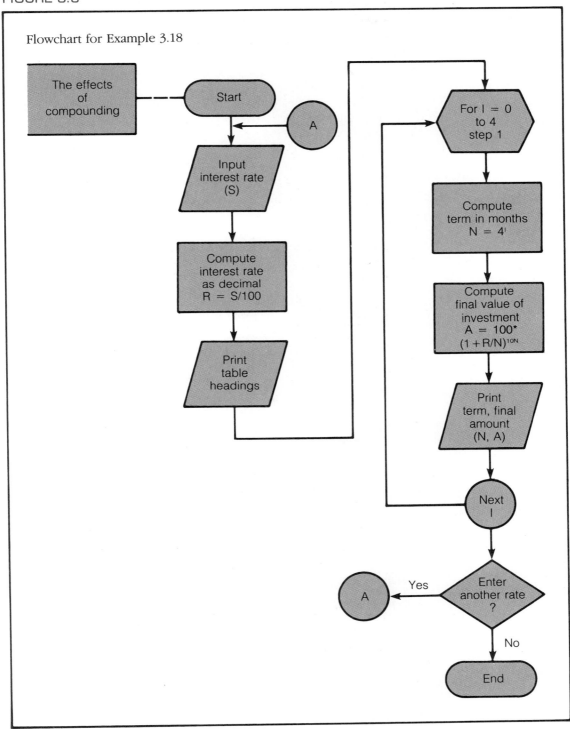

2. Perform calculations

Do

    Prompt, input, and validate S

    Compute R = S / 100

    Print S, principal ($100), and term (10 years)

    For N = 1, 4, 16, 64, 256

        Compute A = $100 * (1 + R / N)^{(10 * N)}$

        Print N and A

    End For

Until user wants to quit

We will implement the For loop in step 2 by

    For I = 0, 1, 2, 3, 4

        Compute N = $4 \char`^ I$

The only question remaining is what form the output shall take. We will print a table like this:

TIMES PER YEAR COMPOUNDED	INVESTMENT VALUE
1	XXX.XX
4	XXX.XX
16	XXX.XX
64	XXX.XX
256	XXX.XX

PROGRAM CODE

```
100 REM    **   COMPOUND INTEREST DEMONSTRATION   **
110 REM             S. VENIT        MARCH, 1987
120 REM
130 REM    THIS PROGRAM SHOWS THE EFFECT OF VARIOUS COMPOUNDING
140 REM    RATES ON THE VALUE OF AN INVESTMENT.  IT MAKES USE OF
150 REM    THE COMPOUND INTEREST FORMULA FOR THE CALCULATIONS.
160 REM
170 REM    VARIABLES:
180 REM        A ...... FINAL VALUE OF THE INVESTMENT
190 REM        R, S ... RATE OF INTEREST AS DECIMAL, PERCENT
200 REM
210    CLS
220    PRINT "           THE EFFECTS OF COMPOUNDING"
230    PRINT
240    PRINT "WHEN YOU ENTER AN INTEREST RATE, THIS PROGRAM"
250    PRINT "WILL COMPUTE THE VALUE OF AN INVESTMENT OF $100"
260    PRINT "AFTER 10 YEARS USING SEVERAL RATES OF COMPOUNDING"
270 REM
280 REM REPEAT CALCULATIONS IF USER DESIRES
290 REM
300        PRINT
310 REM
320 REM    REPEAT UNTIL INTEREST RATE IS GREATER THAN 1
330 REM
340        PRINT "ENTER A RATE OF INTEREST AS A PERCENT."
350        INPUT S
360        PRINT
```

```
370             IF S <= 1 THEN 320
380             LET R = S / 100
390             PRINT
400 REM
410 REM     PRINT HEADINGS
420 REM
430             PRINT "AMOUNT INVESTED:    $100"
440             PRINT "INTEREST RATE:      "; S; "  PERCENT"
450             PRINT "INVESTMENT TERM:    10   YEARS"
460             PRINT
470             PRINT "TIMES PER YEAR"; TAB(19); "INVESTMENT"
480             PRINT " COMPOUNDED";    TAB(19); " VALUE"
490             PRINT "-------------"; TAB(19); "----------"
500 REM
510 REM       COMPUTE AND PRINT INVESTMENT VALUE (ROUNDED)
520 REM
530             FOR I = 0 TO 4
540                LET N = 4 ^ I
550                LET A = 100 * (1 + R / N) ^ (N * 10)
560                PRINT TAB(5); N; TAB(19);
570                PRINT USING "####.##"; A
580             NEXT I
590 REM
600             PRINT
610             PRINT "ENTER ANOTHER RATE? (Y/N)"
620             INPUT R$
630         IF R$ = "Y" THEN 280
640 REM
650 REM   END CALCULATION LOOP
660 REM
670        END
```

PROGRAM TEST

A test run of this program looks like this:

```
                    THE EFFECTS OF COMPOUNDING

        WHEN YOU ENTER AN INTEREST RATE, THIS PROGRAM
        WILL COMPUTE THE VALUE OF AN INVESTMENT OF $100
        AFTER 10 YEARS USING SEVERAL RATES OF COMPOUNDING

        ENTER A RATE OF INTEREST AS A PERCENT.
        ? 10


        AMOUNT INVESTED:    $100
        INTEREST RATE:      10   PERCENT
        INVESTMENT TERM:    10   YEARS

        TIMES PER YEAR      INVESTMENT
          COMPOUNDED          VALUE
        - - - - - - - -     - - - - - -
             1               259.37
             4               268.51
            16               270.99
            64               271.61
           256               271.77

        ENTER ANOTHER RATE? (Y/N)
        ? Y
```

```
ENTER A RATE OF INTEREST AS A PERCENT.
? 20


AMOUNT INVESTED:   $100
INTEREST RATE:      20    PERCENT
INVESTMENT TERM:    10    YEARS

TIMES PER YEAR     INVESTMENT
   COMPOUNDED         VALUE
- - - - - - - - - -  - - - - - - - - -
       1             619.17
       4             704.00
      16             729.81
      64             736.59
     256             738.37

ENTER ANOTHER RATE? (Y/N)
? N
```

REVIEW EXERCISES

Short Answer

1. Let $A = 3$ and $A\$ = $ "NO". Which of the following expressions are true? Which are false?

   a. $(A \wedge 2) > (-A \wedge 2)$

   c. A$ <> "NO"

   b. $(2 * A + 1) <= 7$

   d. A$ = " NO "

2. Which of the following are not fundmental control structures?

   a. A loop structure

   c. A sequential structure

   b. A computation structure

   d. A decision structure

3. Choose the statement that is true for a Do While type loop.

   a. Its test condition is at the bottom of the loop.

   b. It must be executed at least once.

   c. It can be implemented by IF ... THEN and GOTO statements.

   d. It cannot be used to sum a list of numbers.

4. Choose the statement that is true for a FOR/NEXT loop.

   a. The initial value must be less than the limit value.

   b. The loop parameters must be integers.

   c. The control variable must be a numeric one.

   d. The loop increment must be positive.

Debugging

5. Correct the errors in each segment of code.

   a. ```
   300   FOR K = 1 TO 5
   310   FOR J = 1 TO K
   320   PRINT K + J
   330   NEXT K
   340   NEXT J
   ```

   b. ```
   400    LET S = 0
   410    FOR X = 1 TO 10
   420       LET S = S + X
   430    PRINT S
   ```

6. Correct the syntax errors, if any, in each statement.

   a. `500    IF X1 <= (X2^3−3) THEN 300`

   b. `550    IF Z$ = 5.1 THEN 350`

   c. `600    IF N − 2 ≠ 0 THEN 390`

   d. `650    WHILE Z$ = "NOTHING" DO`

7. The following program segment is supposed to average the numbers input by the user. It contains errors in logic. Correct them. (The sentinel value is −99999.)

   ```
   100 REM    **    ALL WRONG    **
   110    LET S = 0
   120    LET C = 0
   130       PRINT "ENTER A NUMBER"
   140       INPUT N
   150       LET C = C + 1
   160       LET S = S + N
   170    IF N <> −99999 THEN 130
   180    LET A = S / N
   190    PRINT "AVERAGE: "; A
   200    END
   ```

8. Run the following program segments. What is the effect of the FOR/NEXT loop in Program B?

   ```
   100 REM    PROGRAM A          100 REM    PROGRAM B
   110    PRINT "HI"             110    PRINT "HI"
   120    PRINT "BYE"            120 REM
   130    END                    130       FOR I = 1 TO 5000
                                  140       NEXT I
                                  150 REM
                                  160    PRINT "BYE"
                                  170    END
   ```

Skill Builders

What is the output of each program segment?

9. ```
   200    FOR I = 7 TO 10 STEP 2
   210       PRINT I;
   220    NEXT I
   230    PRINT I
   ```
   ```

10.
```
200    FOR J = 3 TO 1 STEP -1
210        PRINT J
220        FOR K = 4 TO 3
230            PRINT K
240        NEXT K
250    NEXT J
```

11.
```
200    LET N = 10
210    WHILE N >= 0
220        PRINT N
230        LET N = N - 3
240    WEND
250    PRINT N
```

12.
```
200    LET S = 0
210    FOR I = 1 TO 3
220        LET S = S - I
230    NEXT I
240    PRINT S / (I - 1)
```

13.
```
200        PRINT "ENTER N"
210        INPUT N
220    IF N > 0 THEN 200
230    PRINT N
```
Input: ? 5
   ? −5

14.
```
200    LET S = 0
210    INPUT N
220    IF N = -1 THEN 260
230        LET S = S + N
240        INPUT N
250    GOTO 220
260    PRINT S
```
Input: ? 7
   ? −5
   ? −1

15. a. Write the code in exercise 11 using a Do Until loop.

   b. Write the code in exercise 13 using a Do While loop.

16. a. Write the code in exercise 11 using a FOR/NEXT loop.

   b. Write the code in exercise 9 using an IF/GOTO loop.

PROGRAMMING PROBLEMS

Write a BASIC program to solve each of the following problems. Follow the principles of the software development cycle and use good programming style.

1. Find the sum of the squares of the integers from M to N, where M and N are input by the user.

2. Find the average of the squares of the first N positive integers, where N is input by the user.

3. Allow the user to enter a sequence of temperatures in degrees Celsius terminated by −999. For each one, find the corresponding temperature in degrees Fahrenheit. Remember: The formula is $F = 9C/5 + 32$.

4. Read a list of employee names and ages from DATA statements (terminated by Z, 0) and find the average employee age.

5. Joe Sherman is a baseball fanatic. He would like to have a computer program that figures a player's batting average and slugging percentage. Input to the program would be the player's name and the number of at bats (AB), singles (S), doubles (D), triples (T), and home runs (HR). After the last player has been processed, Joe should enter Z for player name. Batting average (BA) and slugging percentage (SP) are computed by

    BA = (S + D + T + HR) / AB

    and

    SP = (S + 2 * D + 3 * T + 4 * HR) / AB

6. Burt Einstein teaches a math class at Podunk University. It is the end of the semester and Burt needs a progrm that will find each student's average test score as well as the average for the entire class. Input (from DATA statements) the number of tests given and each student's name and test scores. (The last DATA statement should contain ZZZ for student name.) Output the student names and averages as well as the class average.

7. The Archenemy Accounting firm specializes in income tax returns. They would like to have a program that computes the yearly depreciation of a client's assets using the straight line method, whose formula is depreciation = (cost − salvage value)/useful life. The program should input the asset name, cost, salvage value, and useful life and output these items in addition to the yearly depreciation. After each asset is processed, it should ask whether the user wishes to continue.

8. Modify the program in problem 7 so that the output takes the form of a table for each asset.

YEAR	YEARLY DEPRECIATION	ACCUMULATED DEPRECIATION	CURRENT VALUE OF ASSET
1	XXXX.XX	XXXX.XX	XXXX.XX
2	.	.	.
.	.	.	.
.			
N	◄──── Useful life		

DECISIONS

One of a computer's characteristic qualities is its ability to make decisions, to select from among several alternative blocks of code during program execution. These blocks of code, together with the condition that determines which of them is selected, make up a **decision structure.** In this chapter, we will discuss several types of decision structures, the way they are implemented in BASIC, and some of their uses.

4.1 THE IF THEN DECISION STRUCTURE

In the last chapter, we used the IF ... THEN statement for the sole purpose of constructing loops. Here, we will introduce a generalized form of this statement and use it to create a simple decision structure.

The IF ... THEN Statement Revisited

Almost all BASIC dialects contain a general form of the IF ... THEN statement, which was introduced in chapter 3.

The IF ... THEN statement (general form)

Form   IF condition THEN statement

Action   Executes statement if the condition is true; otherwise, skips statement (and executes the next one).

Example   `200   IF X > 0 THEN PRINT "EUREKA!"`

Note: If statement is GOTO xxx, we obtain the "old" version of IF ... THEN (and GOTO may be omitted).

The following example provides a simple illustration of the generalized IF ... THEN statement:

EXAMPLE 4.1   This segment of code determines whether or not an input number is positive.

```
200      INPUT "ENTER A NUMBER ---> ", X
210      PRINT "THE NUMBER "; X; "IS ";
220      IF X <= 0 THEN PRINT "NOT ";
230      PRINT "POSITIVE!"
```

The input number is echo-printed by statement 210. If it is positive, the condition in statement 220 is false and the word *NOT* is not printed. In this case, a run would look like this:

```
ENTER A NUMBER ---> 7
THE NUMBER  7 IS POSITIVE!
```

However, if the input number is negative or zero, the condition in statement 220 is true and the word *NOT* is printed. Typical output for this case would look like this:

```
ENTER A NUMBER ---> -3
THE NUMBER -3 IS NOT POSITIVE!
```

The If Then Structure

Example 4.1 demonstrates how we can execute or skip a single statement depending on whether or not a condition is true. However, sometimes we want to *conditionally* skip a larger block of code. To do this, we simply branch around it. The next example demonstrates this technique.

EXAMPLE 4.2   At some universities, a computer program is used to keep track of information about faculty members. This information might include the faculty member's name; number of publications; and, if he or she holds a doctorate, the university and year of issue. The following program segment could provide input for such a program:

```
400      PRINT "ENTER NAME"
410      INPUT FACNAME$
420      PRINT "DOES FACULTY MEMBER HOLD A DOCTORATE? (Y/N)"
430      INPUT R$
440 REM
450 REM   IF RESPONSE IS NOT 'YES', SKIP NEXT TWO QUESTIONS
460 REM
470      IF R$ <> "Y" THEN 530
480          PRINT "ENTER UNIVERSITY THAT AWARDED IT"      ←— Then
490          INPUT UNIV$                                        Clause
500          PRINT "ENTER YEAR OF ISSUE"
510          INPUT YEAR
520 REM END IF
530 REM
540      PRINT "ENTER NUMBER OF PUBLICATIONS"
550      INPUT NUM
```

The IF ... THEN statement in line 470 determines whether or not the block of code from lines 480 to 510 (the **Then Clause**) is executed. If the response to the question posed on line 420 is Y, then it *is* executed; if the response is anything else, it is not. In the latter case, the IF ... THEN statement causes us to branch around the Then Clause by transferring control to line 530. (Line 470, the statement that determines whether or not the branch occurs, is called a **branch point** of the program.)

The output of two runs through this code looks like this:

Run 1

```
ENTER NAME
? I.S. SMART
DOES FACULTY MEMBER HOLD A DOCTORATE? (Y/N)
? N                                                      Then Clause
                                                         skipped
ENTER NUMBER OF PUBLICATIONS
? 234
```

Run 2

```
ENTER NAME
? N.S. SMART
DOES FACULTY MEMBER HOLD A DOCTORATE? (Y/N)
? Y                                                      Then Clause
                                                         executed
ENTER UNIVERSITY THAT AWARDED IT
? PODUNK U.
ENTER YEAR OF ISSUE
? 1917
ENTER NUMBER OF PUBLICATIONS
? 0
```

A control structure, like the one in example 4.2, which executes a block of code if and only if a given condition is true is called an **If Then decision structure,** or a **single-alternative decision structure.** A flowchart of this structure and the pseudocode we will use to describe it are given in figure 4.1.

NOTE   In BASIC, if we want to execute a series of statements when a given condition is *true*, we use code like the following:

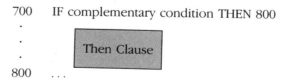

```
700     IF complementary condition THEN 800
  .
  .                     Then Clause
  .
800     ...
```

Here, *complementary condition* is the opposite (or negation) of the *given* condition. For example, if we want to execute a Then Clause when a variable X is positive, then line 700 would read

```
700     IF X <= 0 THEN 800
```

the negation of >

FIGURE 4.1

The If Then Decision Structure

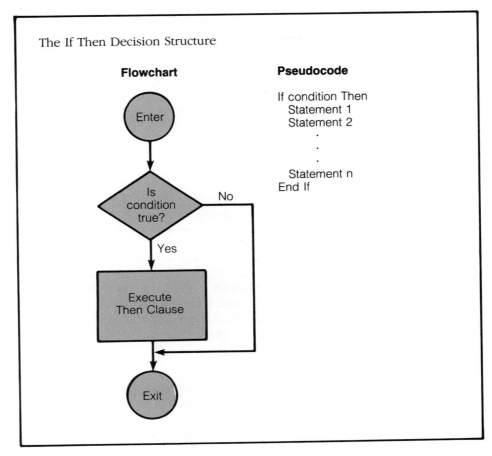

Similarly, to create the negation of some other condition, replace < by >= or replace = by <>, and vice versa.

STYLE POINTER   Identify an If Then Structure

To improve the readability of your programs, you should:

1. Precede an If Then structure by a blank REM statement.

2. Indent the Then Clause.

3. End the structure with REM END IF and a blank REM statement.

4. Identify it by a comment if its meaning is not obvious.

Poor	Better

```
200   IF A >= 10 THEN 230      200  REM
210   PRINT I                  210       IF A >= 10 THEN 250
220   LET J = I ^ 2            220           PRINT I
230   PRINT J                  230           LET J = I ^ 2
                               240  REM END IF
                               250  REM
```

4.2 LOGICAL OPERATORS

In programming, decision making involves testing a *condition* (or *relational expression*). To construct this condition, we use *relational* and *logical operators*. We have discussed the former in section 3.2; we will discuss the latter here.

The most important **logical operators** in BASIC are OR, AND, and NOT. They can be used to create a single *(compound)* condition from two or more *simple* ones. This is illustrated in the next few examples. The truth table for these operators is given in figure 4.2.

EXAMPLE 4.3   The following program segments are functionally equivalent. They both check that the number input lies between 5 and 10.

```
200        PRINT "ENTER A NUMBER BETWEEN 5 AND 10"
210        INPUT X
220   IF X <= 5 THEN 200
230   IF X >= 10 THEN 200

300        PRINT "ENTER A NUMBER BETWEEN 5 AND 10"
310        INPUT X
320   IF (X <= 5) OR (X >= 10) THEN 300
```

In this example, the compound condition

$(X <= 5)$ OR $(X >= 10)$

is true if and only if *either* of the simple conditions

$X <= 5$ or $X >= 10$

is true. It is false if *both* simple conditions are false.

EXAMPLE 4.4   Let A = 1 and B = 2. Which of the following conditions is true? Which is false?

a. (A > B) OR (B > A)

b. (A < 1) OR (B < 1) OR (A*B > 2)

FIGURE 4.2

Truth Tables for OR, AND, and NOT

Let X and Y represent simple conditions. Then for the values of X and Y given on each line at the left of the table, the values of X OR Y, X AND Y, and NOT X are as listed on the right.

X	Y	X OR Y	X AND Y	NOT X
true	true	true	true	false
true	false	true	false	false
false	true	true	false	true
false	false	false	false	true

For a.: We evaluate each simple condition. The first $(A > B)$ is false and the second $(B > A)$ is true. Since at least one of them is true, the given (compound) condition is true.

For b.: Here, we have three simple conditions. The compound condition will be true if and only if at least one of these is true. However, all the simple conditions are false. Hence, so is the given compound condition.

The AND operator also creates a compound condition from two simple ones. For example:

```
              Compound  condition
        ⎧‾‾‾‾‾‾‾‾‾‾‾‾‾‾‾‾‾‾‾‾‾‾‾‾⎫
600  IF (2*X+3 >= 7) AND (A-B <> 1) THEN 650
        ⎩_____⎭    ⎩_____⎭
          Simple  conditions
```

The compound condition created is true if *both* simple conditions are true and is false otherwise.

The NOT operator, unlike OR and AND, acts upon a single condition. For example:

```
830    IF NOT (A <= 6) THEN 870
```

We say that the NOT operator *complements* a given condition; if the condition is true, its complement is false, and vice versa.

EXAMPLE 4.5

Let $A = 1$ and let $B = 2$. Are the following conditions true or false?

a. `((2*A+6) > (B+1)) AND ((B/3) = 1)`

b. `NOT(A*B <> 1)`

For a.: We evaluate each simple condition. Since $2*A + 6 = 8$ is greater than $B + 1 = 3$, the first is true. But $(B/3)$ is not 1, so the second simple condition is false. Since *both* simple conditions must be true for the given compound condition to be true, the latter is false.

For b.: Here, A∗B = 2, so A∗B <> 1 is true. Hence, its complement, NOT(A∗B <> 1), is false.

Hierarchy of Operations

In a relational expression, there may be arithmetic, relational, and logical operations. If parentheses are present, perform the operations within the parentheses first. In the absence of parentheses, do the arithmetic operations first (in their usual order); then any relational operation; and finally, NOT, AND, and OR, in that order. This order of precedence, or hierarchy, of operations is shown in detail in table 4.1.

TABLE 4.1   HIERARCHY OF BASIC OPERATIONS

TYPE	OPERATOR	ORDER PERFORMED
Arithmetic	$\begin{cases} \wedge \\ *, / \\ +, - \end{cases}$	First
Relational	=, <>, <, <=, >, >=	
Logical	$\begin{cases} \text{NOT} \\ \text{AND} \\ \text{OR} \end{cases}$	Last

EXAMPLE 4.6   Let Q = 3 and let R = 5. Is the following relational expression true or false?

```
NOT Q > 3 OR R < 3 AND Q - R < 0
```

Let us insert parentheses to explicitly show the order in which the operations are to be performed.

First   Second

(NOT(Q > 3)) OR ((R < 3) AND ((Q − R) < 0))

Third

If we evaluate the simple conditions first, we learn that Q > 3 is false; R < 3 is false; and (Q − R) < 0 is true. Then, by substituting these values into the relational expression and performing the operations, we can get the answer. A simple way to show this is with an evaluation chart.

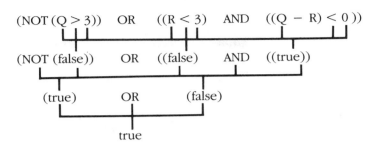

4.3   THE IF THEN ELSE DECISION STRUCTURE

In section 4.1, we discussed the If Then decision structure. Here, we will consider an extension of this idea: the If Then Else structure, which allows for the selection of one of two alternative blocks of code. We say that If Then Else is a dual-alternative decision structure.

The If Then Else Structure

The **If Then Else decision structure,** or **dual-alternative decision structure,** has the form indicated in figure 4.3. If the given condition is true, Block 1 is executed and Block 2 is skipped. If the condition is false, the reverse occurs.

The following code is a simple example of an If Then Else structure. It consists of an IF ... THEN statement to test the condition (X = 0) and two blocks of code called the Then Clause (lines 230 and 240) and the **Else Clause** (line 260).

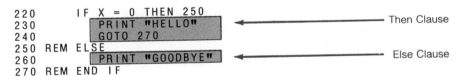

```
220        IF X = 0 THEN 250
230              PRINT "HELLO"                                    Then Clause
240              GOTO 270
250   REM ELSE
260              PRINT "GOODBYE"                                  Else Clause
270   REM END IF
```

If X is zero, the condition in statement 220 is true and control is transferred to line 250. Thus, the Then Clause is skipped and the Else Clause executed: GOODBYE is displayed on the screen. On the other hand, if X is *not* zero, the condition is false and the Then Clause is executed, displaying HELLO. In this case, the GOTO statement (line 240) causes a branch to line 270 and the Else Clause is skipped.

The next example contains an If Then Else structure nested within a loop.

EXAMPLE 4.7   This program finds the average of all positive and of all negative numbers input by the user.

```
100   REM   **   AVERAGING POSITIVE AND NEGATIVE NUMBERS   **
110   REM               S. VENIT          APRIL, 1987
120   REM
130   REM   THIS PROGRAM INPUTS A LIST OF NUMBERS AND FINDS THE
140   REM   AVERAGE OF THE POSITIVE AND OF THE NEGATIVE NUMBERS.
```

FIGURE 4.3

The If Then Else Decision Structure

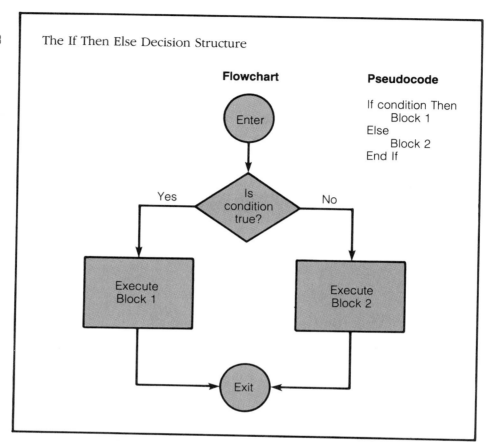

Flowchart

Pseudocode

```
If condition Then
      Block 1
Else
      Block 2
End If
```

```
150 REM
160 REM      VARIABLES:
170 REM          AP, AN ... AVERAGE OF POSITIVE, NEGATIVE NUMBERS
180 REM          CP, CN ... COUNT OF POSITIVE, NEGATIVE NUMBERS
190 REM          N ........ NUMBER INPUT
200 REM          SP, SN ... SUM OF POSITIVE, NEGATIVE NUMBERS
210 REM
220     CLS
230     PRINT "THIS PROGRAM FINDS THE AVERAGE OF THE POSITIVE"
240     PRINT "  AND OF THE NEGATIVE NUMBERS THAT YOU INPUT."
250     PRINT
260 REM
270 REM     INITIALIZE COUNTERS AND ACCUMULATORS
280 REM
290     LET CP = 0
300     LET CN = 0
310     LET SP = 0
320     LET SN = 0
330 REM
340     PRINT "ENTER A NUMBER.  (ENTER  0  TO QUIT.)"
350     INPUT N
360 REM
370 REM     SUM POSITIVE AND NEGATIVE NUMBERS
380 REM
390     WHILE N <> 0
```

```
400 REM
410         IF N < 0 THEN 450
420             LET CP = CP + 1
430             LET SP = SP + N                              Then Clause
440             GOTO 480
450 REM     ELSE
460             LET CN = CN + 1                              Else Clause
470             LET SN = SN + N
480 REM     END IF
490 REM
500             PRINT "ENTER ANOTHER NUMBER OR 0 TO QUIT."
510             INPUT N
520         WEND
530 REM
540 REM     COMPUTE AND PRINT AVERAGES
550 REM
560         LET AP = SP / CP
570         LET AN = SN / CN
580         PRINT
590         PRINT "THE AVERAGE OF THE POSITIVE NUMBERS IS "; AP
600         PRINT "THE AVERAGE OF THE NEGATIVE NUMBERS IS "; AN
610 REM
620         END
```

In this program, we use an end-of-file loop (lines 390–520) with sentinel value 0 to do the necessary summing. The If Then Else structure (lines 410–480) lies within this loop. If N is positive, the Then Clause (lines 420–440) is executed and the GOTO statement in line 440 causes the Else Clause (lines 460–470) to be skipped. If N is negative, the Then Clause is skipped and the Else Clause is executed. In this way, the proper accumulator and counter are incremented in each pass through the loop.

NOTE   If we want a Then Clause to be executed when a given condition is true, then we must use the complement of this condition in the IF ... THEN statement. (This was also the case for the If Then structure of section 4.1.) For example, in example 4.7, the Then Clause is to be executed if N is positive. To do this, we use the relational expression (line 410), N < 0.

Thus, in BASIC, an If Then Else control structure has the form

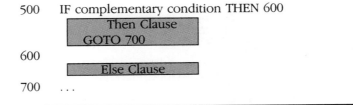

```
500     IF complementary condition THEN 600
                    Then Clause
                    GOTO 700
600
                    Else Clause
700     . . .
```

An If Then Else control structure should be isolated from the code above it by a blank REM statement. If the structure's purpose is not obvious, it should also be preceded by a step comment. The Then and Else Clauses should be indented and separated from one another by a REM ELSE comment. Finally, the Else Clause should be followed by a REM END IF comment.

Poor	**Better**

```
200    IF X > 5 THEN 230      200 REM
210    PRINT X + 2            210     IF X > 5 THEN 240
220    GOTO 240               220         PRINT X + 2
230    PRINT X — 2            230         GOTO 260
240    . . .                  240 REM ELSE
                              250         PRINT X — 2
                              260 REM END IF
```

Defensive Programming

The program in example 4.7 contains a flaw. If no positive numbers are input, the counter CP will remain 0 and a "division by 0" error will occur in line 560, causing execution to terminate at this point. If no negative numbers are input, this problem will occur in line 570. To prevent program execution from halting prematurely—to prevent a *crash*—in these cases, we must program defensively.

Defensive programming is the inclusion of code within a program to check during execution for improper data. The code that catches and reports the error is called an **error trap.** (One aspect of defensive programming, data validation, has already been discussed in section 3.3.)

EXAMPLE 4.8

To prevent a possible "division by 0" error in line 560 or 570 of example 4.7 (caused by a zero value for counters CP or CN), we change the end of the program to read:

```
540 REM    COMPUTE AND PRINT AVERAGES
550 REM
560    IF CP <> 0 THEN 590
570        PRINT "THERE ARE NO POSITIVE NUMBERS IN THE DATA."
580        GOTO 620
590 REM ELSE
600        LET AP = SP / CP
610        PRINT "THE AVERAGE OF THE POSITIVE NUMBERS IS "; AP
620 REM END IF
630    IF CN <> 0 THEN 660
640        PRINT "THERE ARE NO NEGATIVE NUMBERS IN THE DATA."
650        GOTO 690
660 REM ELSE
670        LET AN = SN / CN
680        PRINT "THE AVERAGE OF THE NEGATIVE NUMBERS IS "; AN
690 REM END IF
700    END
```

By checking CP (in line 560), we determine whether or not there were any positive numbers among the data. The first If Then Else structure (lines 560–620) then causes the proper action to take place. Similarly, the second If Then Else structure (lines 630–690) handles the negative number case.

The IF ... THEN ... ELSE Statement

Some BASIC dialects contain an IF ... THEN ... ELSE statement to implement the If Then Else decision structure. We will discuss the Microsoft BASIC version of this statement. The general form of the IF ... THEN ... ELSE statement in Microsoft BASIC (for the IBM PC, Macintosh, TRS-80, and other computers) follows:

The IF ... THEN ... ELSE statement (Microsoft BASIC)

Form   IF condition THEN statement 1 ELSE statement 2

Action   If condition is true, statement 1 is executed; otherwise statement 2 is executed.

Example   ```200 IF ANS$ = "Y" THEN PRINT "HI" ELSE PRINT "HO"```

Note: Statement 1 or statement 2 (or both) can be line numbers, in which case a transfer of control takes place when that "statement" is selected.

EXAMPLE 4.9   The following program segment counts the number of positive and the number of negative numbers input by the user.

```
200      LET CP = 0
210      LET CN = 0
220      INPUT "ENTER A NUMBER ---> ", X
230 REM
240      WHILE X <> 0
250         IF X > 0 THEN LET CP = CP + 1 ELSE LET CN = CN + 1
260         INPUT "ENTER ANOTHER NUMBER (0 TO QUIT) ---> ", X
270      WEND
```

This program segment contains a standard end-of-file loop (with sentinel value 0) for counting the numbers. The IF ... THEN ... ELSE statement within the loop determines whether the number input is positive or negative and increments the appropriate counter.

NOTE   In Microsoft BASIC, the keyword LET is optional. Hence, statement 250 of example 4.9 can be written

```
250      IF X > 0 THEN CP = CP + 1 ELSE CN = CN + 1
```

We can increase the power of the IF ... THEN ... ELSE statement by taking advantage of Microsoft BASIC's *line formatting* features.

Multistatement Lines. Several statements can be written on a single line if they are separated by colons (:). For example:

```
350      LET X = 0: LET Y = 0: LET Z = 0
360      IF X = 0 THEN LET X = X + 1: PRINT Y; Z
```

Multiline Statements. A single statement (or series of statements separated by colons) can span several lines as long as the total number of characters used does not exceed 255. (Since blanks count, this amounts to a little more than three 80-character lines.) Only one line number, at the beginning of the statement, is used in this case.

When you reach the end of one line, to move the cursor to the beginning of the next, hold down the Control key and press Enter. Do *not* press the Enter key alone to move to the next line of a multiline statement.

As an illustration of this feature, let us return to line 250 of example 4.9. This code looks a little nicer if it is written

```
250      IF X > 0 THEN LET CP = CP + 1  ◀────── Hold down Control
                     ELSE LET CN = CN + 1         and press Enter
```

4.4   SELECTING FROM SEVERAL ALTERNATIVES

The If Then Else decision structure (section 4.3) selects one of two alternative blocks of code. Sometimes our programs must contain decisions having more than two alternatives. In this situation, we use a **Case decision structure,** also called a **multiple-alternative decision structure.** It can be implemented in BASIC in several ways.

Chaining If Then Structures

One way to handle multiple alternatives is to use a sequence (or *chain*) of If Then structures. If the alternatives are simple enough, IF ... THEN *statements* will suffice.

EXAMPLE 4.10   The following code might appear in a student grade program. It converts letter grades, L$, to numerical grades earned, useful later in calculating grade point averages.

```
500      IF L$ = "A" THEN LET NGE = 4
510      IF L$ = "B" THEN LET NGE = 3
520      IF L$ = "C" THEN LET NGE = 2
530      IF L$ = "D" THEN LET NGE = 1
540      IF L$ = "F" THEN LET NGE = 0
```

The five statements allow for the five possible letter grades. Since only one of the five conditions can be true, this code selects the proper alternative and assigns the corresponding numerical grade.

The structure created in example 4.10 is simple but not very efficient. Even if the first alternative is selected, all five statements will be executed. Using a sequence of If Then *structures* is generally more efficient and allows for more complicated alternatives. It does, however, require more code.

EXAMPLE 4.11
This program segment is a modification of the one in example 4.10. It uses If Then *structures* and contains an error trap.

```
600        IF L$ <>"A" THEN 630
610            LET NGE = 4
620            GOTO 810
630 REM ELSE
640        IF L$ <>"B" THEN 670
650            LET NGE = 3
660            GOTO 810
670 REM ELSE
680        IF L$ <>"C" THEN 710
690            LET NGE = 2
700            GOTO 810
710 REM ELSE
720        IF L$ <>"D" THEN 750
730            LET NGE = 1
740            GOTO 810
750 REM ELSE
760        IF L$ <>"F" THEN 790
770            LET NGE = 0
780            GOTO 810
790 REM ELSE THERE IS AN ERROR
800        PRINT "ILLEGAL GRADE"
810 REM END IF
```

Here, the IF ... THEN statements (lines 600, 640, 680, 720, and 760) are executed in succession *until* one of the conditions is false. Then, the corresponding Then Clause is executed, which assigns the proper numerical grade and transfers control to the end of the structure. If execution reaches line 800, the letter grade was not A, B, C, D, or F. This statement reports that fact. The flowchart in figure 4.4 shows the logic of this structure.

The ON ... GOTO Statement

In the previous examples, the code has gone through a sequence of decisions. Ideally, a Case decision structure should contain only *one* decision-making statement which alone selects the proper alternative. The ON ... GOTO statement does just this.

FIGURE 4.4

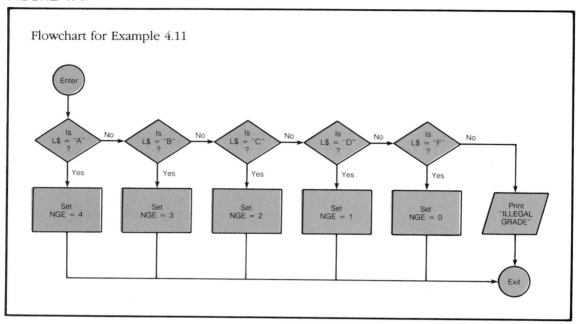

Flowchart for Example 4.11

The ON ... GOTO statement

Form   ON numeric expression GOTO ln1, ln2, ...
where ln1, ln2, ... denote line numbers

Action   Evaluates the numeric expression (rounding if necessary)
to get an integer *n*; then transfers control to the *n*th line
number listed.

Examples   200   ON K GOTO 400, 500, 650, 720
250   ON 2 * X + 1 GOTO 440, 550, 620

EXAMPLE 4.12   This example illustrates the use of the ON ... GOTO statement.

```
100 REM    ***    AREA COMPUTER   ***
110 REM    S. VENIT         APRIL, 1987
120 REM
130 REM    THIS PROGRAM COMPUTES THE AREA OF A CIRCLE, TRIANGLE
140 REM    OR RECTANGLE AT THE USER'S OPTION.
150 REM
160 REM    VARIABLES:
170 REM        A ........ AREA OF THE FIGURE
180 REM        B, H ..... BASE AND ALTITUDE OF THE TRIANGLE
190 REM        L, W ..... LENGTH AND WIDTH OF THE RECTANGLE
200 REM        R ........ RADIUS OF THE CIRCLE
210 REM
220 REM    CONSTANT:
```

```
230 REM          PI = 3.1416 (THE VALUE OF PI)
240 REM
250     CLS
260     PRINT "                 AREA COMPUTER"
270     PRINT
280 REM
290 REM REPEAT UNTIL USER SELECTS A "LEGAL" OPTION
300 REM
310         PRINT "IF YOU WANT TO FIND:"
320         PRINT "    THE AREA OF A CIRCLE, ENTER ....... 1"
330         PRINT "    THE AREA OF A RECTANGLE, ENTER .... 2"
340         PRINT "    THE AREA OF A TRIANGLE, ENTER ..... 3"
350         PRINT
360         INPUT N
370     IF N < 1 OR N > 3 THEN 290
380 REM
390 REM     SELECT PROPER ALTERNATIVE
400 REM
410     ON N GOTO 430, 560, 690
420 REM
430 REM    CASE 1 ---------- CIRCLE --------------------------
440 REM
450 REM REPEAT UNTIL RADIUS IS POSITIVE
460         PRINT "ENTER RADIUS OF CIRCLE."
470         INPUT R
480         PRINT
490     IF R <= 0 THEN 450
500 REM
510     LET PI = 3.1416
520     LET A = PI * R * R
530     PRINT "THE AREA OF THE CIRCLE WITH RADIUS"; R; "IS"; A
540     GOTO 810
550 REM
560 REM    CASE 2 ---------- RECTANGLE ------------------------
570 REM
580 REM REPEAT UNTIL BOTH LENGTH AND WIDTH ARE POSITIVE
590         PRINT "ENTER THE LENGTH AND WIDTH OF THE RECTANGLE."
600         INPUT L, W
610         PRINT
620     IF L <= 0 OR W <= 0 THEN 580
630 REM
640     LET A = L * W
650     PRINT "THE AREA OF THE RECTANGLE WITH DIMENSIONS"
660     PRINT "     "; L; "AND"; W; "IS"; A
670     GOTO 810
680 REM
690 REM    CASE 3 ------------ TRIANGLE -----------------------
700 REM
710 REM REPEAT UNTIL BASE AND HEIGHT ARE POSITIVE
720         PRINT "ENTER THE BASE AND HEIGHT OF THE TRIANGLE."
730         INPUT B, H
740         PRINT
750     IF B <= 0 OR H <= 0 THEN 710
760 REM
770     LET A = B * H / 2
780     PRINT "THE AREA OF THE TRIANGLE WITH BASE"; B; "AND"
790     PRINT "          HEIGHT"; H; "IS" A
810 REM ------------------- END OF CASES -------------------
820 REM
830     END
```

The text displayed by lines 310–350 is called a **menu;** it lists the options available to the user. (We will discuss menus in more detail in chapter 5.) The number chosen is assigned to a variable, N, and then used in the ON ... GOTO statement (line 410) to select the proper alternative. When this statement is executed:

If N = 1, control transfers to the first line number (430).
If N = 2, control transfers to the second line number (560).
If N = 3, control transfers to the third line number (690).

(On most systems, if N is either 0 or greater than 3, the next statement in the program will be executed. In our program, the error trap in line 370 ensures that N is in the proper range.)

The block of code (or *case*) selected by the ON ... GOTO statement is then executed, printing the desired area. Notice that GOTO statements at the end of the first two cases (lines 540 and 670) cause a branch around the remaining case(s). No branch is needed at the end of the third case. A flowchart showing the logical structure of the ON ... GOTO statement in this program is shown in figure 4.5.

STYLE POINTER   Identify a Case Structure

To improve the readability of your programs, type your multiple-alternative decision structure so that the individual cases are easily identified. You can do this by using blank REM statements before and after each case. Moreover, if the purpose of any case is not immediately apparent, precede it by a step comment as well. (See example 4.12.)

4.5   FOCUS ON PROBLEM SOLVING

This section provides a detailed application of the material you learned in this chapter.

Determining Sales Commissions

EXAMPLE 4.13   The Custom Cabinet Company figures the monthly sales commissions for its employees in the following way:

8 percent on all sales for the month;
an additional 4 percent on sales over $15,000; and
an additional 2 percent on sales over $30,000.

The CCC wants to feed its sales data into a computer program to determine the commissions of its three salespersons: Thomas, Richard, and Harriet. Each sale would be recorded in a DATA statement of the form:

SALESPERSON, INVOICE NUMBER, DATE OF SALE, AMOUNT OF SALE

FIGURE 4.5

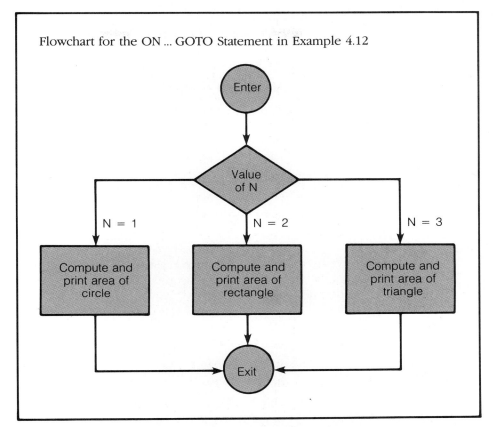

Flowchart for the ON ... GOTO Statement in Example 4.12

The sentinel record would take the form:

Z, 0, 0/0, 0

The only user input to the program is to be the month and year of the reporting period. The output should be a table listing each salesperson's name, total sales, and total commissions.

PROBLEM ANALYSIS

The input variables are

    Month and year of the report: MONTH$ and YEAR

    Salesperson, invoice number, date, and amount for each sale: S$, NUM, DT$, and AMT

The output variables are

    Total sales and commission: S and C

To compute the commission, we use the formulas:

    If $S < 15{,}000$ then $C = S * 0.08$

    If $S >= 15{,}000$ but $S < 30{,}000$ then $C = S * 0.08 + (S - 15{,}000) * 0.04$

    If $S >= 30{,}000$ then $C = S * 0.08 + (S - 15{,}000) * 0.04$

        $+ (S - 30{,}000) * 0.02$

PROGRAM DESIGN

An initial pseudocode outline of this program follows:

1. Clear screen and print title

2. Input month and year of report (MONTH$, YEAR)

3. Print the report headings

4. For each salesperson

    4.1 Read data (S$, NUM, DT$, AMT)

    4.2 Sum sales, S

    4.3 Compute commission, C

    4.4 Print name, sales, and commission

    End For

You'll notice that our outline now contains subnumbers (4.1, 4.2, 4.3, and 4.4). We will use this format in our pseudocode to help us identify different levels when we need to develop them further.

Now we'll develop steps 3 and 4 of this outline in more detail.

3. Print the report headings

    3.1 Print title of company

    3.2 Print MONTH$, YEAR

    3.3 Print table headings: SALESPERSON   SALES   COMMISSION

4. For I = 1, 2, 3

    If I = 1 Then set salesperson = "THOMAS"

    If I = 2 Then set salesperson = "RICHARD"

    If I = 3 Then set salesperson = "HARRIET"

    4.1 Read data (S$, NUM, DT$, AMT)

    4.2 Sum sales, S

      4.2.1 Initialize S to 0

      4.2.2 Do While not EOF   ▸ Use E$ for

          If salesperson = S$ Then   "salesperson"

          Increment S by AMT

          Read S$, NUM, DT$, AMT

          End If

        End While

    4.3 Compute commission, C

      4.3.1 Set C = S * 0.08

      4.3.2 If S > 15,000 Then increment C by (S − 15,000) * 0.04

      4.3.3 If S > 30,000 Then increment C by (S − 30,000) * 0.02

4.4 Print name, sales, and commission

End For

A flowchart for our design of this program is given in figure 4.6.

FIGURE 4.6

Flowchart for Example 4.13

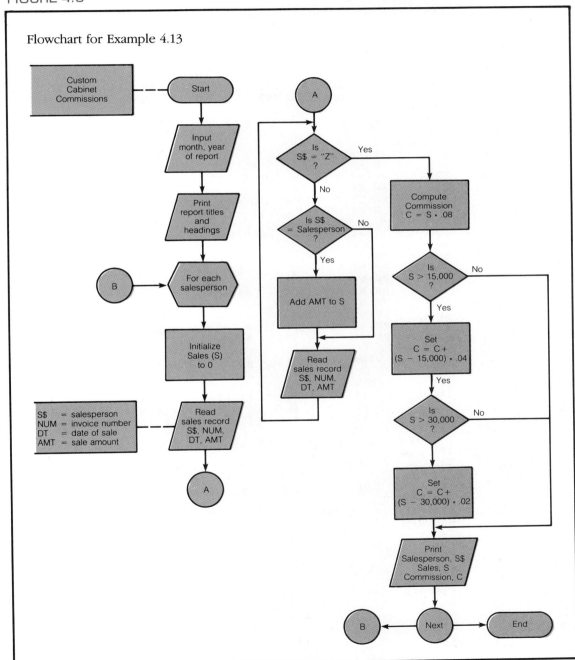

PROGRAM CODE

When we code the program, we include DATA statements that will help to test it.

```
100 REM    **    CUSTOM CABINET COMMISSIONS    **
110 REM
120 REM        S. VENIT           APRIL, 1987
130 REM
140 REM    THIS PROGRAM COMPUTES THE COMMISSION ON SALES
150 REM    FOR SEVERAL SALESPERSONS.
160 REM
170 REM    VARIABLES:
180 REM       C .............. TOTAL COMMISSIONS
190 REM       E$ ............. EMPLOYEE NAME
200 REM       MONTH$, YEAR .... MONTH AND YEAR OF REPORT
210 REM       NUM, DT$, AMT ... INVOICE NUMBER, DATE AND AMOUNT
220 REM                            OF SALE
230 REM       S$ ............. SALESPERSON MAKING SALE
240 REM       S .............. TOTAL SALES
250 REM
260     CLS
270     PRINT "          CUSTOM CABINET COMPANY"
280     PRINT "        SALES COMMISSION CALCULATOR"
290     PRINT
300     PRINT "ENTER MONTH AND YEAR OF REPORT."
310     INPUT MONTH$, YEAR
320 REM
330 REM    PRINT REPORT HEADINGS
340 REM
350     CLS
360     PRINT "          CUSTOM CABINET COMPANY"
370     PRINT
380     PRINT "          SALES REPORT — "; MONTH$; YEAR
390     PRINT
400     PRINT
410     PRINT "SALESPERSON", "TOTAL SALES", "COMMISSION"
420     PRINT "----------", "----------", "----------"
430 REM
440 REM    FOR EACH SALESPERSON, COMPUTE COMMISSION
450 REM
460     FOR I = 1 TO 3
470        IF I = 1 THEN LET E$ = "THOMAS"
480        IF I = 2 THEN LET E$ = "RICHARD"
490        IF I = 3 THEN LET E$ = "HARRIET"
500 REM
510 REM       INITIALIZE TOTAL SALES FOR EACH SALESPERSON
520 REM
530        LET S = 0
540 REM
550        READ S$, NUM, DT$, AMT
560 REM
570 REM       WHILE NOT EOF, PROCESS DATA RECORD
580 REM
590        WHILE S$ <> "Z"
600           IF S$ = E$ THEN LET S = S + AMT
610           READ S$, NUM, DT$, AMT
620        WEND
630 REM
640 REM       COMPUTE AND PRINT COMMISSION
650 REM
660        LET C = S * .08
670        IF S > 15000 THEN LET C = C + (S — 15000) * .04
680        IF S > 30000 THEN LET C = C + (S — 30000) * .02
690        PRINT E$,
```

```
700          PRINT USING "$$#####.##  "; S; C
710          RESTORE
720      NEXT I
730 REM
740 REM      SALESPERSON   NUMBER    DATE    AMOUNT
750 REM
760      DATA  HARRIET,     5673,    5/7,     4000.00
770      DATA  THOMAS,      5674,    5/9,     3000.00
780      DATA  HARRIET,     5675,    5/9,    12000.00
790      DATA  THOMAS,      5676,    5/14,    1000.00
800      DATA  RICHARD,     5677,    5/18,   20000.00
810      DATA  HARRIET,     5678,    5/21,   24000.00
820      DATA  Z,           0,       0/0,     0
830 REM
840      END
```

PROGRAM TEST

To see if the program is running properly, we must use DATA that result in testing the three branches of the commission computation: total sales less than 15,000, total sales between 15,000 and 30,000, and total sales greater than 30,000. The DATA statements listed in the program do this. Moreover, since the resulting total sales are, in each case, round numbers, we can easily check that the proper commission is obtained.

A sample run of the programs gives the output:

```
            CUSTOM CABINET COMPANY
          SALES COMMISSION CALCULATOR

ENTER MONTH AND YEAR OF REPORT.
? MAY, 1987


            CUSTOM CABINET COMPANY

          SALES REPORT — MAY 1987


SALESPERSON    TOTAL SALES    COMMISSION
-----------    -----------    ----------
THOMAS         $4,000.00        $320.00
RICHARD        $20,000.00     $1,800.00
HARRIET        $40,000.00     $4,400.00
```

REVIEW EXERCISES

Short Answer

1. Let A = 2, B = 5, and C$ = "HERE". Determine whether the given relational expressions are true or false.

   a. A ^ 3 — 7 = 0 OR NOT (B = 3)

   b. C$ <> "HER" AND (A * B < 0 OR NOT (C$ = "HERE"))

2. Choose the one attribute that does *not* apply to the ON ... GOTO statement.

   a. It can be used to implement some If Then Else structures.

   b. It can contain variables in the list of line numbers.

   c. It can always be replaced by a sequence of If Then structures.

   d. It can contain a numeric expression between ON and GOTO.

3. Which of the following is *not* a decision structure?

   a. A Case structure

   b. A sequential structure

   c. A single-alternative structure

   d. An If Then Else structure

Debugging

Correct the logic errors in the given program segments so that they run correctly.

4. This program segment is supposed to print HELLO if N$ = "ALONSO" and print GOODBYE otherwise.

```
300      IF N$ = "ALONSO" THEN 320
310          PRINT "HELLO"
320 REM ELSE
330          PRINT "GOODBYE"
340 REM END IF
```

5. This program segment is supposed to print the sign of a given number X as −1 if X < 0, 0 if X = 0, and 1 if X > 0.

```
400      ON X + 1 GOTO 410, 440, 470
410 REM
420      PRINT "−1"
430      GOTO 470
440 REM
450      PRINT "0"
460      GOTO 490
470 REM
480      PRINT "1"
490 REM
```

6. Correct the syntax errors in each of the following statements:

   a. `800    ON X − 1 GOTO 40, N, M`

   b. `850    IF X <> 1 OR < 3) THEN 880`

7. Correct the syntax error in the following Microsoft BASIC statement:

```
500      IF X > 0 THEN PRINT "+"
510              ELSE PRINT "−"
```

Skill Builders

What is displayed when each of the program segments in exercises 8–11 is run?

```
8.  200     LET X = 5
    210     IF X > 0 THEN PRINT X
    220     IF NOT(X = 0 OR X < 0) THEN PRINT X ^ 2
    230     IF X ^ 2 >= 0 AND 2 * X — 1 <> 0 THEN PRINT X + 1
```

```
9.  200     INPUT K
    210     IF K <= 0 THEN 250
    220         PRINT "1"
    230         LET K = K + 1
    240         GOTO 270
    250         PRINT "2"
    260         LET K = K — 1
    270     PRINT K
```

a. Assume input is 10

b. Assume input is −10

```
10. 200     INPUT R
    210     ON R — 1 GOTO 220, 240, 260
    220     PRINT "1"
    230     GOTO 270
    240     PRINT "2"
    250     GOTO 270
    260     PRINT "ERROR"
    270     PRINT "BYE"
```

a. Assume input is 2

b. Assume input is 3

```
11. 200     INPUT X, Y
    210     IF X < Y THEN PRINT X: PRINT "IS SMALL"
            ELSE PRINT Y: PRINT "IS OK"
```

a. Assume input is 1, 2

b. Assume input is 2, 1

12. Write code containing an ON ... GOTO statement corresponding to the flow-chart in figure 4.7.

PROGRAMMING PROBLEMS

Write BASIC programs to solve the following problems:

1. Find and print the largest of a list of numbers entered by the user and terminated by −9999.

FIGURE 4.7

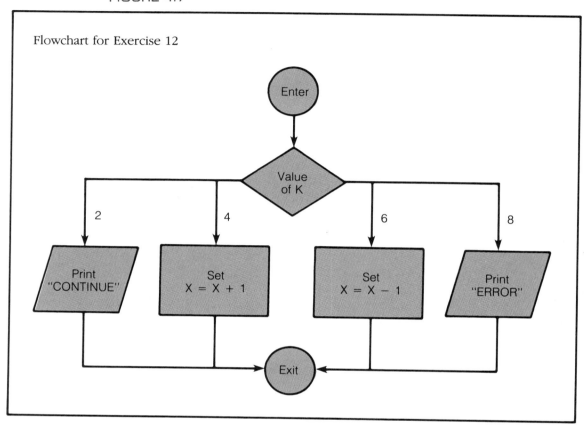

Flowchart for Exercise 12

2. Find and print the smallest of a set of numbers listed in DATA statements and terminated by 9999. Test your program using:

DATA   −2, 10, 0, −5, 1, 9999

3. Find the change from a dollar for a purchase that costs less than a dollar. Give the change in the largest denomination coins (half-dollars, quarters, dimes, nickels, and pennies) possible.

4. Compute the income tax due on a taxable income input by the user according to the following table:

TAXABLE INCOME		TAX DUE	OF AMOUNT OVER
FROM	TO		
23,500	28,800	4,115 + 30%	23,500
28,800	34,100	5,705 + 34%	28,800
34,100	41,500	7,507 + 38%	34,100
41,500	55,300	10,319 + 42%	41,500
55,300	81,800	16,115 + 46%	55,300
81,800	------	28,835 + 50%	81,800

5. Input two numbers and, at the user's option, find their sum, difference, product, or quotient. Use a menu in your program. (See example 4.12 to refresh your memory about menus.)

6. Input a list of numbers, terminated by 0, and at the user's option, find their sum, their average, or the sum of their squares. Use a menu in your program (see example 4.12).

7. The Bountiful Bagel Bakery has two locations, one in East Southgate (ES) and one in South Eastgate (SE). They want to feed the figures for their weekly bagel sales into a computer program which will print a sales report for each location. This report should list (for each store) the types of bagels sold (plain, onion, and sesame) and total sales and revenue for each type of bagel. The plain, onion, and sesame bagels sell for 20, 25, and 30 cents a piece, respectively. The report should also include the total revenue for each store.

   The weekly bagel sales are to be given in DATA statements that contain the following information:

LOCATION	TYPE	NUMBER SOLD
SE	Plain	2,345
SE	Onion	4,782
SE	Sesame	3,339
ES	Plain	1,268
ES	Sesame	3,872
ES	Onion	3,335

8. For the Bountiful Bagel Bakery of problem 7, create just one sales report of the type described. It should be for the location that has the greatest total sales.

MODULAR PROGRAMMING

In this chapter, we will introduce the concept of modular programming. You will learn the principles of modular programming and how to implement them in BASIC by the use of subroutines.

5.1   PROGRAM MODULES AND HIERARCHY CHARTS

Every program consists of a number of programming tasks that must be performed to solve the underlying problem. In this section, we will introduce the concept of a **program module:** an independent, self-contained block of code that performs a single task. **Modular programming** is the process of designing and coding a program as a set of interrelated modules.

The Modular Programming Method

"Divide and conquer" is a basic technique for solving large and complicated problems. To apply this method, the given problem is broken down into smaller, more manageable subproblems. These are then studied and, if need be, further subdivided. Eventually (we hope), the subproblems created by this process will be simple enough to solve one at a time. We then backtrack, combining the partial results into a solution for the original problem.

Modular programming is the application of this technique to program design. To design a program in a modular fashion, we first determine the major programming tasks. Each of these is viewed as a program module, a program within a program (or a **subprogram**). Some of these modules may be broken into submodules, which in turn may contain submodules of their own, and so on. After determining all the modules needed to solve the given problem (as well as the relationships among them), we design each of them using pseudocode or by developing a flowchart.

A logical question to ask at this point is: How do I know when to stop breaking the submodules into more submodules? This leads us to the more basic question: What makes a module a module? To answer the first question by way of the second, let us list the characteristics of a module:

1. A module performs a single task. For example, an *input module* prompts, inputs, and validates the given data.

2. A module is self-contained and independent of other modules. This implies that, like a control structure, it has only one entry and one exit point.

3. A module is not too long. Ideally, its code should not exceed one page (about 60 lines) in length. Since this allows one to see all the code at once, it greatly enhances readability.

The modular design approach has the following advantages over a nonmodular one:

1. Program readability is improved. This in turn reduces the time needed for debugging and maintaining the program.

2. Programmer productivity is increased because it is easier to design, code, and test the program one module at a time than all at once.

3. The various program modules can be designed and/or coded by different programmers, an essential feature in large, complex programs.

4. In some cases, a single module can be used at more than one place in the program. This reduces the total amount of code within the program.

5. Modules performing common programming tasks (such as sorting) can be used in more than one program. These *utility modules* reduce both design and coding time.

STYLE POINTER   Write Modularized Programs

If your program runs more than a page or two in length, separate it into modules by using subprograms. This will greatly enhance readability. The larger the program, the greater the benefit.

Hierarchy Charts

To keep track of all the program modules and the relationships among them, we will use **hierarchy charts.** A hierarchy chart describes these relationships in the same way that an organization chart determines who's responsible to whom in a business firm.

Figure 5.1 depicts a typical hierarchy chart. At the top of the chart is the **main module** (think of it as the "chairman of the code"). It is here that program execution will begin. All other program modules are subprograms of the main module. In addition, some modules (for example, Modules B1 and B2 in figure 5.1) are subprograms of other modules.

In section 5.3, we will further demonstrate how hierarchy charts are used in the design process.

5.2 BASIC SUBROUTINES

In section 5.1, we discussed the concept of writing a program as a collection of *modules*. This idea is implemented in BASIC by the use of subprograms called **subroutines.**

The GOSUB and RETURN Statements

To *call* a subroutine into action in BASIC, we use a GOSUB statement. This statement (like GOTO) causes an unconditional transfer of control to a specified line number: the first statement of the subroutine. At the end of the subroutine, a

FIGURE 5.1

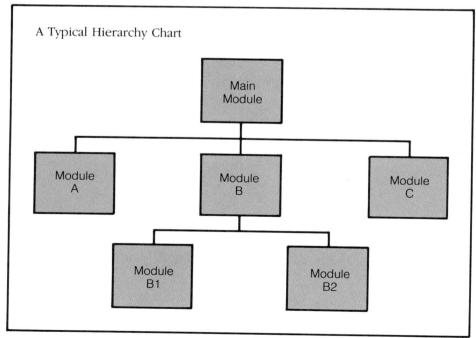

A Typical Hierarchy Chart

RETURN statement transfers control back to the line immediately following the GOSUB. The action of these statements is illustrated in the following example:

EXAMPLE 5.1

```
100 REM     **   GOSUB/RETURN EXAMPLE   **
110 REM     S. VENIT           JUNE, 1987
120 REM
130 REM     THIS PROGRAM DISPLAYS A MESSAGE INPUT BY THE USER.
140 REM
150 REM     SUBROUTINE USED:
160 REM         LINEDRAW ..... PRINTS A LINE OF ASTERISKS
170 REM
180 REM     VARIABLES:
190 REM         N ........ NUMBER OF ASTERISKS IN THE LINE DRAWN
200 REM         TEXT$ .... THE MESSAGE
210 REM
220     CLS
230     PRINT "ENTER THE MESSAGE TO BE DISPLAYED."
240     INPUT TEXT$
250     LET N = 50
260 REM
270 REM     CALL "LINEDRAW"
280 REM
290     GOSUB 500
300     PRINT TEXT$
310 REM
320 REM     CALL "LINEDRAW"
330 REM
340     GOSUB 500
350     STOP
360 REM
500 REM     **********   SUBROUTINE LINEDRAW   **********
510 REM
520 REM     THIS SUBROUTINE PRINTS A ROW OF ASTERISKS
530 REM
540 REM     VARIABLE:
550 REM         I ....... CONTROL VARIABLE OF FOR LOOP
560 REM
570     PRINT
580     PRINT
590     FOR I = 1 TO N
600        PRINT "*";
610     NEXT I
620     PRINT
630     PRINT
640     PRINT
650 REM
660     RETURN
670 REM
999     END
```

In this program, the first GOSUB 500 (in statement 290) transfers control to the subroutine beginning at line 500. After skipping two lines, the subroutine prints 50 (the value of N) asterisks. Then, two more lines are skipped (the first PRINT, statement 620, just moves the cursor to the beginning of a new line). When the RETURN statement is executed, control is transferred to statement 300, the line immediately following the GOSUB that caused the call to the subroutine.

The text input by the user is now printed. Then, another GOSUB 500 in line 340 causes the subroutine to be executed again. This time, the RETURN statement transfers control to line 350 and the STOP statement terminates execution of the program. (If STOP were not there, execution would continue into the subroutine again.)

A typical run of this program looks like this:

```
ENTER THE MESSAGE TO BE DISPLAYED.
? THE QUICK BROWN FOX JUMPED OVER THE LAZY DOG.


*****************************************************

THE QUICK BROWN FOX JUMPED OVER THE LAZY DOG.


*****************************************************

Break in 350
```

NOTE   The message "Break in 350" in example 5.1 is a typical one displayed when the STOP statement is executed. If you want to avoid this somewhat unsightly text from appearing in your output, you could do one of two things:

1. Replace STOP by END (and eliminate the END in line 999).
2. Replace STOP by GOTO 999.

A variable, like I in example 5.1, that is only used in the subroutine is called a **local variable.** A variable that appears in the main module (like N or TEXT$), even if it is used in the subroutine, is called a **global variable.**

STYLE POINTER   Identify a Program's Subroutines

List the subroutines called by the main module in its header comments (as in lines 150–160 of example 5.1). Moreover, whenever a GOSUB statement appears, precede it by a step comment identifying the subroutine being called. (This is done by statement 320 of example 5.1.)

NOTE   In some BASIC dialects, comments can be placed at the end of a line of code if they are preceded by a special symbol. (In Microsoft BASIC, this symbol is the apostrophe, ' .) Although overuse of this feature may decrease the clarity of a program, it *is* useful in identifying the subroutine being called by a GOSUB statement. For example, instead of writing

```
300 REM
310 REM    CALL THE AVERAGING SUBROUTINE
320 REM
330       GOSUB 600
```

we could simply use

```
300 REM
310       GOSUB 600         'CALL THE AVERAGING SUBROUTINE
```

STYLE POINTER   Use Header Comments in Subroutines

Begin every subroutine with a sequence of REM statements. Give the subroutine's name in the very first line (the one referenced by the GOSUB). Follow this by its purpose, the subprograms called within it, and a list of local variables. Remember: a subroutine is a sub*program*, so treat it like one.

The GOSUB and RETURN statements

Form   GOSUB line number
            RETURN

Action   GOSUB transfers control to the indicated line number;
            RETURN transfers control to the line immediately following
            GOSUB.

Example   ```
200   GOSUB 300
   .
   .
   .
300 REM   BEGIN SUBROUTINE
   .
   .
   .
480   RETURN
```

---

The STOP statement

**Form**       STOP

**Action**    Terminates program execution

**Example**   ```
620    STOP
```

The ON . . . GOSUB Statement

The ON . . . GOSUB statement provides another way to call subroutines in BASIC. It works very much like the ON . . . GOTO statement (see section 4.4), transferring control to the listed line numbers based upon the value of a numeric expression. However, ON . . . GOSUB is used to enter a subroutine, and thus requires a RETURN to transfer control back to the calling module. The general form of this statement follows:

The ON . . . GOSUB statement

Form   ON expression GOSUB ln1, ln2, . . .
                  where expression is a numeric variable or expression; ln1,
                  ln2, . . . are line numbers

Action   Evaluates expression (rounding to an integer if necessary)
                  and branches to the subroutine at the corresponding line
                  number.

Examples   ON K GOSUB 400, 700, 800, 900
                  ON 2 * N — 1 GOSUB 2000, 2500, 3000

EXAMPLE 5.2   This example illustrates the use of the ON . . . GOSUB statement. The program segment calls subroutine ALPHA if N = 1, BETA if N = 2, and GAMMA if N = 3.

```
490         INPUT N
500         ON N GOSUB 600, 700, 800
510         STOP
520 REM
600 REM     **    SUBROUTINE ALPHA    **
     .
     .
     .
680         RETURN
690 REM
700 REM     **    SUBROUTINE BETA    **
     .
     .
     .
780         RETURN
790 REM
800 REM     **    SUBROUTINE GAMMA    **
     .
     .
     .
880         RETURN
```

The value of N in the ON . . . GOSUB statement (line 500) determines which of the listed line numbers (600, 700, or 800) will be used for branching. If N = 1, control is transferred to the first of these; if N = 2, to the second; and if N = 3, to the third. After the appropriate subroutine is executed, its RETURN statement causes a branch back to the line immediately following the ON . . . GOSUB.

NOTE   If the value of the variable or expression in an ON . . . GOSUB statement is 0, then the next statement will be executed. If the value is less than 0 or greater than the length of the list of line numbers, then the resulting action depends upon your version of BASIC. Either the next statement will be executed or an error message will be displayed and the run terminated.

PROGRAMMING POINTER

You should always program defensively when using an ON...GOSUB statement. Use data validation techniques (see section 3.3) to ensure that the value of the expression in your ON...GOSUB statement is in the proper range. For example, the INPUT statement in line 490 of example 5.2 should be placed in a data validation loop:

```
480 REM REPEAT UNTIL NUMBER ENTERED IS VALID
485        PRINT "ENTER EITHER 1, 2, OR 3."
490        INPUT N
495     IF N < 1 OR N > 3 THEN 480
```

This guarantees that the value of N entered is 1, 2, or 3.

STYLE POINTER   Use Distinctive Line Numbers to Begin Subroutines

The reader will have an easier time locating the subroutine being called if its first line number is distinctive. For example, in a program using four-digit line numbers, you might use those that are multiples of 500 (like 2500 or 3000) to begin your subroutines. (In example 5.2, with its three-digit line numbers, 600, 700, and 800 are used for this purpose.)

5.3   FOCUS ON PROBLEM SOLVING

In this section, we will design and code a program that illustrates the topics covered in this chapter. We will use the techniques of modular programming to create a **menu-driven program,** one that displays the options available to the user in the form of a *menu* (see section 4.4).

A Student Data Base Problem

EXAMPLE 5.3   The dean of the School of Mathematical Sciences at Near West University has decided it's high time the school computerized its student data base. He has in mind a program that could retrieve student data in different ways. The program would contain a DATA statement for each student, listing:

student name
sex (M or F)
whether undergraduate or graduate (U or G)

major code (1 for Math, 2 for Statistics, 3 for Computer Science)
number of units completed
grade points earned (4 for each A, 3 for each B, and so on)

(The last DATA statement would be a sentinel record.)
The dean would like to use the program to output:

1. A list of all students in a given major (major code input by dean)

2. A Dean's List: all students with a grade point average greater than a specified number (input by dean)

PROBLEM ANALYSIS

The input variables are

Student name and sex (M or F): STU$ and SEX$
Undergraduate or graduate student (U or G): UGCODE$
Major code (1 for Math, 2 for Statistics, 3 for Computer Science): MAJOR
Number of units completed and grade points earned: UNITS and GRPTS
Major code input by user (for creating student list): CODE
Grade point average input by user (for Dean's List): CUTOFF

(Other variables will be necessary to input the user's menu choices.)

The output variable is

Student grade point average: GPA

The one formula is

GPA = GRPTS / UNITS

PROGRAM DESIGN

We will design the program as a menu-driven one using modular programming techniques. Each of the tasks listed in example 5.3 will be coded as a separate subroutine. The hierarchy chart is given in figure 5.2.

Each of the modules is now designed independently using pseudocode (as follows), or a flowcharting technique. In figure 5.3 a new flowchart symbol

is used to represent the action of calling a subroutine.

Main Module

Do While user wishes to continue
    Call MENU subroutine to display main menu

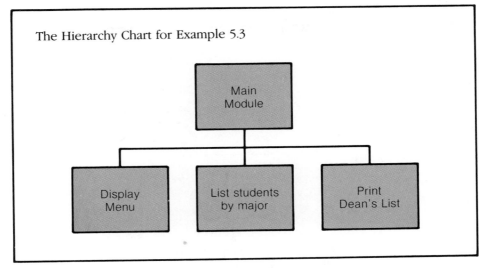

FIGURE 5.2   The Hierarchy Chart for Example 5.3

> Input user selection
>> Call appropriate subroutine: MAJ LIST or DEAN
> End While

End Main Module

MENU Module

> Print main menu selections
>> (Print list of majors, Print Dean's List, and Terminate program)

End MENU module

MAJOR LIST module

> Input user's selection of major to be listed (CODE)
> Read initial student record
> Do While not end-of-file
>> If CODE = MAJOR Then Print student name End If
>> Read another record
> End While

End MAJOR LIST Module

DEAN'S LIST Module

> Input cutoff GPA for Dean's List (CUTOFF)
> Read initial student record
> Do While not end-of-file
>> Compute GPA = GRPTS / UNITS
>> If GPA >= CUTOFF Then Print student name, GPA End If
>> Read another record
> End While

End DEAN'S LIST Module

FIGURE 5.3

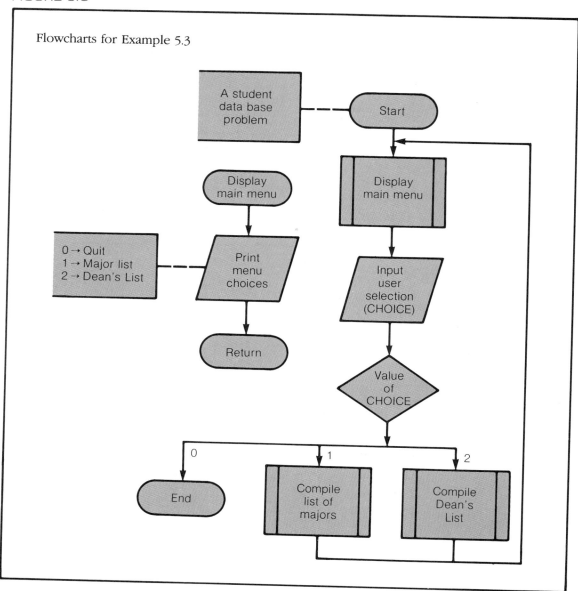

Flowcharts for Example 5.3

FIGURE 5.3

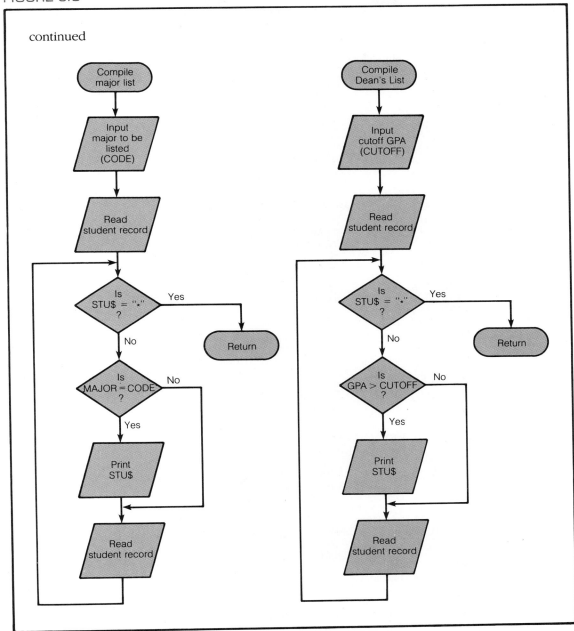

PROGRAM CODE

Each module in figure 5.2 is coded as a subroutine called by an ON...GOSUB statement. Notice that in coding the program, additional detail has been added to the design. This includes clear screen statements, validation of all user input, and RESTORE statements at the end of subroutines to allow the data to be reused by another module.

```
1000 REM   ***********************************************************
1010 REM   *                   STUDENT DATA BASE                     *
1020 REM   *                                                         *
1030 REM   *       S. VENIT                    JUNE, 1987            *
1040 REM   *                                                         *
1050 REM   *   THIS PROGRAM CONTAINS A LIST OF STUDENTS AND INFOR-   *
1060 REM   *   MATION ABOUT EACH.   IT ALLOWS FOR THE RETRIEVAL OF   *
1070 REM   *   THIS INFORMATION IN SEVERAL WAYS (SEE MAIN MENU).     *
1080 REM   *                                                         *
1090 REM   *   SUBROUTINES (OF MAIN MODULE):                         *
1100 REM   *      MENU ....... DISPLAYS MAIN MENU                    *
1120 REM   *      DEAN ....... PRINTS "DEAN'S LIST"                  *
1130 REM   *      MAJ LIST ... LISTS STUDENTS IN GIVEN MAJOR         *
1140 REM   *                                                         *
1150 REM   *   GLOBAL VARIABLES:                                     *
1160 REM   *      CHOICE ..... USER MENU SELECTION                   *
1170 REM   *      GRPTS ...... GRADE POINTS EARNED                   *
1180 REM   *      MAJOR ...... MAJOR CODE (1 = MATH, 2 = STAT,       *
1190 REM   *                                      3 = CS)            *
1200 REM   *      SEX$ ....... EITHER 'M' OR 'F'                     *
1205 REM   *      STU$ ....... STUDENT NAME                          *
1210 REM   *      UGCODE$ .... 'U' FOR UNDERGRADS, 'G' FOR GRADS     *
1220 REM   *      UNITS ...... NUMBER OF UNITS COMPLETED             *
1230 REM   ***********************************************************
1240 REM
1250 REM   ******************  MAIN MODULE  *********************
1260 REM
1270 REM   RUN PROGRAM UNTIL USER WISHES TO QUIT
1280 REM
1290       LET CHOICE = 1
1300       WHILE CHOICE <> 0
1310 REM
1320 REM      REPEAT UNTIL USER SELECTS VALID CHOICE
1330            GOSUB 2000
1340            INPUT CHOICE
1350          IF CHOICE < 0 OR CHOICE > 2 THEN 1320
1360 REM
1370 REM          DEPENDING ON CHOICE, CALL MAJ LIST OR DEAN
1380 REM
1390          ON CHOICE GOSUB 4000, 5000
1400       WEND
1410 REM
1420       STOP
1430 REM
2000 REM   ****************  SUBROUTINE MENU  ****************
2010 REM
2020 REM   THIS SUBROUTINE DISPLAYS THE MAIN MENU.
2030 REM
2040       CLS
2050       PRINT "              STUDENT DATA BASE"
2060       PRINT
2070       PRINT
2080       PRINT "     TO QUIT ...................... ENTER 0"
2100       PRINT "     TO LIST STUDENTS BY MAJOR ........ ENTER 1"
2110       PRINT "     TO PRINT DEAN'S LIST ............ ENTER 2"
2120 REM
```

```
2130       RETURN
2140 REM
4000 REM    **************   SUBROUTINE MAJ LIST   ****************
4010 REM
4020 REM       THIS SUBROUTINE PRINTS A LIST OF THE STUDENTS IN THE
4030 REM                 MAJOR INPUT BY THE USER.
4040 REM
4050 REM       VARIABLE:
4060 REM          CODE ...... MAJOR CODE ENTERED BY USER
4070 REM
4080 REM REPEAT UNTIL VALID CODE IS ENTERED BY USER
4090           CLS
4100           PRINT "FOR A LIST OF THE STUDENTS IN A MAJOR, ENTER"
4110           PRINT "          THE MAJOR CODE"
4120           PRINT
4130           PRINT "     FOR MATHEMATICS ................. ENTER 1"
4140           PRINT "     FOR STATISTICS ................... ENTER 2"
4150           PRINT "     FOR COMPUTER SCIENCE ............ ENTER 3"
4160           INPUT CODE
4170       IF CODE < 1 OR CODE > 3 THEN 4080
4180 REM
4190 REM       LIST STUDENTS IN SPECIFIED MAJOR
4200 REM
4210       CLS
4220       READ STU$, SEX$, UGCODE$, MAJOR, UNITS, GRPTS
4230 REM
4240       WHILE STU$ <> "*"
4250          IF MAJOR = CODE THEN PRINT STU$
4255          READ STU$, SEX$, UGCODE$, MAJOR, UNITS, GRPTS
4260       WEND
4270 REM
4280       PRINT
4290       PRINT "TO RETURN TO MAIN MENU, PRESS 'ENTER'."
4300       INPUT ANSWER$
4310 REM
4320       RESTORE
4330       RETURN
4340 REM
5000 REM    ****************   SUBROUTINE DEAN   ***************
5010 REM
5020 REM       THIS SUBROUTINE INPUTS A GRADE POINT AVERAGE (GPA)
5030 REM       AND PRINTS A LIST OF ALL STUDENTS WHOSE GPA IS
5040 REM                 GREATER THAN THIS NUMBER.
5050 REM
5060 REM       VARIABLES:
5070 REM          CUTOFF ..... CUTOFF POINT ENTERED BY USER
5080 REM          GPA ........ STUDENT'S GRADE POINT AVERAGE
5090 REM
5150 REM REPEAT UNTIL VALID CUTOFF POINT IS ENTERED
5160           CLS
5170           PRINT "    ENTER A NUMBER BETWEEN 0 AND 4 TO"
5180           PRINT "OBTAIN A LIST OF ALL STUDENTS WHOSE GPA"
5190           PRINT "          EXCEEDS THIS NUMBER."
5200           INPUT CUTOFF
5210       IF CUTOFF < 0 OR CUTOFF > 4 THEN 5150
5220 REM
5230 REM       LIST STUDENTS WITH GPA >= CUTOFF
5240 REM
5250       CLS
5260       READ STU$, SEX$, UGCODE$, MAJOR, UNITS, GRPTS
5270       WHILE STU$ <> "*"
5280 REM
5290          IF UNITS = 0 THEN LET GPA = 0
                       ELSE LET GPA = GRPTS / UNITS

5300 REM
```

```
5310              IF GPA >= CUTOFF THEN PRINT STU$, GPA
5315           READ STU$, SEX$, UGCODE$, MAJOR, UNITS, GRPTS
5320      WEND
5330 REM
5340      PRINT
5350      PRINT "TO RETURN TO MAIN MENU, PRESS 'ENTER'."
5360      INPUT ANSWER$
5370 REM
5380      RESTORE
5390      RETURN
5400 REM
6000 REM   *****************   DATA BLOCK   *********************
6010 REM
6020 REM           NAME         SEX    UG/G    MAJOR   UNITS    GRPTS
6030 REM
6040      DATA  T. ALLISON,     M,      U,       1,      45,       98
6050      DATA  A. CLANCY,      M,      U,       2,     112,      342
6060      DATA  R. ESTAVEZ,     F,      U,       3,      73,      275
6070      DATA  K. JONES,       M,      G,       1,      15,       42
6080      DATA  N. JONES,       F,      G,       2,      21,       80
6090      DATA  L. MARTIN,      F,      G,       3,      18,       72
6100      DATA  A. PHILLIPS,    M,      U,       3,      34,       60
6110      DATA  R. SMITH,       M,      U,       3,      79,      240
6120      DATA  A. THOMAS,      F,      U,       2,      55,      110
6130      DATA  R. WONG,        M,      G,       3,       9,       27
6140      DATA  O. ZIZZIL,      F,      U,       1,       0,        0
6150      DATA  * ,             *,      *,       0,       0,        0
6160 REM
9999      END
```

PROGRAM TEST

A typical run of this program looks like this:

```
            STUDENT DATA BASE


      TO QUIT .......................... ENTER 0
      TO LIST STUDENTS BY MAJOR ........ ENTER 1
      TO PRINT DEAN'S LIST ............. ENTER 2
  ? 1
```

```
   FOR A LIST OF THE STUDENTS IN A MAJOR, ENTER
              THE MAJOR CODE

      FOR MATHEMATICS ................. ENTER 1
      FOR STATISTICS .................. ENTER 2
      FOR COMPUTER SCIENCE ............ ENTER 3
  ? 1
```

```
┌─────────────────────────────────────────────────────┐
│                                                       │
│   T. ALLISON                                          │
│   K. JONES                                            │
│   O. ZIZZIL                                           │
│                                                       │
│   TO RETURN TO MAIN MENU, PRESS 'ENTER'.              │
│   ?                                                   │
│                                                       │
└─────────────────────────────────────────────────────┘
```

```
┌─────────────────────────────────────────────────────┐
│                                                       │
│              STUDENT DATA BASE                        │
│                                                       │
│      TO QUIT ........................... ENTER 0      │
│      TO LIST STUDENTS BY MAJOR ........ ENTER 1       │
│      TO PRINT DEAN'S LIST ............. ENTER 2       │
│   ? 0                                                 │
│   Break in 1420                                       │
│                                                       │
└─────────────────────────────────────────────────────┘
```

REVIEW EXERCISES

Short Answer

1. Which of the following is not a characteristic of a program module?

   a. It performs only a single task.

   b. It appears only in menu-driven programs.

   c. It is independent of the other modules.

   d. It is relatively short in length.

2. Which of the following is not an advantage of modular programming?

   a. It improves program readability.

   b. It results in programs that are shorter in length.

   c. It makes the design of the program easier.

   d. It results in programs that are easier to test and debug.

3. Which of the following is true of hierarchy charts?

   a. They show more detail than flowcharts.

   b. They require special symbols for different program actions.

   c. They show the interrelationships among the program modules.

   d. They can be used only in business-related programs.

Debugging

4. Find the syntax errors in each of the following statements:

    a. `200    GOSUB TO 1000`

    b. `210    ON  2 * Y + 3 GOSUB A, B`

Correct the errors in each of the programs in exercises 5 and 6.

5.
```
100 REM    THIS PROGRAM PRINTS A SINGLE WORD: ONE, TWO, OR THREE
110 REM
120        INPUT "ENTER A NUMBER", N
130        ON N GOSUB 200, 300, 400
200        PRINT "ONE"
300        PRINT "TWO"
400        PRINT "THREE"
500 REM
510        END
```

6.
```
100        THIS PROGRAM PRINTS A MESSAGE ENCLOSED IN PARENTHESES
110 REM
120        PRINT "ENTER THE MESSAGE"
130        INPUT TEXT
140        GOSUB 300
150        PRINT TEXT
160        GODUB 400
170 REM
300        PRINT "(";
310 REM END OF SUBROUTINE
400        PRINT ")"
410        RETURN
420        END
```

Skill Builders

What is displayed when each of the program segments in exercises 7–10 is run?

7.
```
200        GOSUB 400
210        GOSUB 500
220        PRINT "ONE"
230        STOP
400 REM
410        PRINT "TWO"
420        RETURN
500 REM
510        PRINT "THREE"
520        RETURN
```

8.
```
200        GOSUB 400
210        PRINT "START"
220        STOP
400 REM
410        PRINT "GOING"
420        GOSUB 500
430        PRINT "STILL GOING"
440        RETURN
500 REM
510        PRINT "GONE"
520        RETURN
```

9.
```
200        LET N = 2
210        ON N GOSUB 400, 300
220        GOTO 999
300        PRINT "IS FUN";
310        RETURN
400        PRINT "BASIC ";
410        RETURN
999        PRINT "?"
```

```
10.  200      LET X = 1
     210      ON X^2 + 1 GOSUB 500, 600, 700
     220      PRINT X
     230      STOP
     500      PRINT 2 * X
     510      RETURN
     600      PRINT 3 * X
     610      RETURN
     700      PRINT 4 * X
     710      RETURN
```

PROGRAMMING PROBLEMS

In problems 1 and 2, write a BASIC subroutine that performs the indicated task.

1. The subroutine inputs (from the user) an employee's name, sex, and hours worked. (Be sure to use the appropriate prompts and data validation.)

2. The subroutine finds the average of a set of numbers (terminated by 0) listed in DATA statements.

In problems 3 and 4, write a menu-driven modular program to solve the given problem.

3. For a set of numbers listed in DATA statements (terminated by 0), at the user's option

    a. find their average; *or*

    b. find the average of the positive ones and the average of the negative ones.

4. The personnel office at The Ultimate Software Company needs a program to print two kinds of reports. The first lists the number of employees of each sex in the following age brackets: under 25, 25–40, and over 40. The second prints the names of those employees of a given sex in an age group specified by the user. Each employee's name, sex, and age will be given in a separate DATA statement. Use the following statements to test your program:

```
DATA  A. AARDVARK,       M,   27
DATA  D. COYOTE,         F,   23
DATA  R. DINOSAUR,       M,   31
DATA  X. ELEPHANT,       M,   43
DATA  T. GHOTI,          F,   37
DATA  Y. HORESTON,       M,   52
DATA  N. PTERODACTYL,    F,   61
DATA  A. RHINO,          M,   24
```

Write a modularized program to solve problems 5 and 6.

5. The registrar at Near West University wants a program to determine the class rank of its students given the number of semester units completed. The pro-

gram should read (from DATA statements) a list of students and the number of units (U) each has completed. (The list will be terminated by Z, 0.) It should then print this information together with the class rank of each student according to the following formula:

$1 <= U < 32$ ....FRESHMAN
$32 <= U < 64$ ....SOPHOMORE
$64 <= U < 96$ ....JUNIOR
$96 <= U < 128$ ....SENIOR

The program should also print the total number of students in each class in bar graph form as illustrated.

```
FRESHMEN      *************** 15
SOPHOMORES    ************ 12
JUNIORS       *** 3
SENIORS       ******************************************** 42
```

6. The Last National Bank has finally decided to computerize its monthly checking account reports. The program should read (from DATA statements) the customer's name, account number, and beginning balance. It should then read a list of transactions for that customer. Each transaction will consist of a code (C for check, D for deposit), the date, and the amount. The list of transactions is terminated by E, 0, 0. The list of customers is terminated Z, 0, 0. For example:

```
800  DATA  JONES, 02345, 28.50
810  DATA  D, 3,  120
820  DATA  C, 14, 23.67
830  DATA  C, 18, 39.21
840  DATA  E, 0,  0
850  DATA  SMITH, 03615, 1024
860  DATA  C, 8,  432.89
870  DATA  C, 23, 2453.99
880  DATA  E, 0, 0
890  DATA  Z, 0, 0
```

If a check overdraws the account (the balance drops below 0), that check should be ignored and a $5 penalty assessed. After each customer's transactions have been processed, 20 cents per check should be deducted from the account.

The output of this program should be, for each customer, the name, the account number, the list of transactions, and a summary. The latter consists of beginning balance, number of checks and deposits, and ending balance.

ARRAYS

In all our programs thus far, a *single* variable (one storage location in internal memory) has been associated with each variable name. In this chapter, we will discuss the concept of an **array:** a *collection* of variables, all of which are referenced by the same name. We will discuss one-dimensional arrays (lists) and two-dimensional arrays (tables), concentrating on the former. You will learn how to set up and use arrays in BASIC programs to accomplish various tasks, including sorting and searching lists of data.

6.1 ONE-DIMENSIONAL ARRAYS

A **one-dimensional array** is a list of related data of the same type (either numbers or strings) referred to by the same variable name. In this section, we will discuss how to set up and manipulate these arrays.

Declaring Arrays

To use an array, we must have some way of referring to the individual variables (or **elements**) contained within it. This is done by means of **subscripts,** integers enclosed in parentheses following the name of the array, as illustrated in our first example.

EXAMPLE 6.1   Suppose we want to input a city's monthly rainfall figures for a given year and store them in memory for processing later in the program. We could do this by assigning the rainfall figures to 12 different variables using code similar to

```
200      READ RAINJAN, RAINFEB, RAINMAR, RAINAPR, RAINMAY, RAINJUN
210      READ RAINJUL, RAINAUG, RAINSEP, RAINOCT, RAINNOV, RAINDEC
         .
         .
         .
```

```
400      DATA  4.32, 4.67, 4.10, 3.42, 3.05, 2.54
410      DATA  2.10, 2.05, 2.78, 3.40, 3.87, 4.15
```

We can achieve the same effect using a single array in the following way:

```
300      FOR K = 1 TO 12
310          READ RAIN(K)
320      NEXT K
         .
         .
         .

400      DATA  4.32, 4.67, 4.10, 3.42, 3.05, 2.54
410      DATA  2.10, 2.05, 2.78, 3.40, 3.87, 4.15
```

In this segment of code, the array is named RAIN and has 12 elements: RAIN(1), RAIN(2), RAIN(3), and so on. (Here, the array *subscripts* are the integers 1, 2, . . . , 12, and we read the array *elements* as "RAIN sub 1", "RAIN sub 2", etc.) On each pass through the FOR/NEXT loop, the rainfall figure for one of the months is read and assigned to the corresponding array element. For example, on the first pass, K = 1, so statement 310 assigns the value 4.32 to RAIN(1); on the second pass, K = 2, so 4.67 is assigned to RAIN(2); and so on, until the last pass (K = 12), when 4.15 is assigned to RAIN(12).

Thus, after this segment of code is executed, the array RAIN may be pictured as shown in figure 6.1. (The variable names are given on the left and their values are boxed in on the right.)

Array elements are also known as **subscripted variables,** whereas our "old" (nonsubscripted) variables are called **simple variables.** Before a subscripted variable can be used in a program, the array to which it belongs must be **declared** (or **dimensioned**): it must be provided with storage space (within the computer's memory) for all its elements. This is done by means of a DIM (for dimension) statement. For example, the second segment of code presented in example 6.1 should be preceded by a statement like this:

```
150      DIM RAIN(12)
```

This statement tells the computer to set aside (or allocate) enough consecutive memory locations to hold the 12 elements of our array RAIN.

The general form of the DIM statement follows. (Notice that we can declare several arrays in a single dimension statement.)

FIGURE 6.1

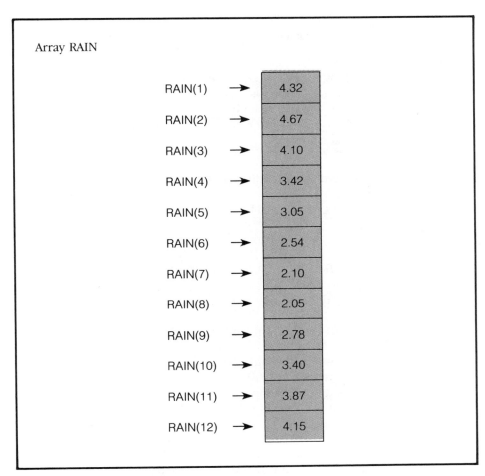

Array RAIN

The DIM (dimension) statement

Form   DIM var1(bound1), var2(bound2), . . .
where var1, var2, . . . are the array names; and bound1,
bound2, . . . are *upper bounds* for the arrays: integer
constants or variables that represent the largest subscripts
permitted

Action   Allocates storage space (in the computer's memory) for the
elements of an array.

Examples 250   DIM X(20)
300   DIM A$(10), TEST(5), STU$(N)

PROGRAMMING POINTER

Every array should be declared before its first use. Otherwise, when the array is referenced, either execution will terminate or the array will automatically be dimensioned with an upper bound of 10 (depending on your version of BASIC). However, even if your system automatically dimensions the array, it is good programming practice to *always* use DIM statements.

In some dialects (including Microsoft BASIC), a statement such as

```
170    DIM TEST(5)
```

will allocate enough memory to store the *six* array elements

TEST(0), TEST(1), TEST(2), TEST(3), TEST(4), and TEST(5)

In other dialects, only *five* locations are set aside

TEST(1), TEST(2), TEST(3), TEST(4), and TEST(5)

In other words, the *lower bound* for the array TEST will be either 0 or 1, depending on your version of BASIC. Nevertheless, even if your system allocates space for an element with subscript 0, you need not use this variable. For example, if the statement

```
150    DIM RAIN(12)
```

is inserted into the segment of code in example 6.1, the code will run on *all* systems.

When a subscripted variable is used in a program, its subscript may be a numeric constant, variable, or expression. Upon execution, its value is rounded or truncated (depending upon the system) to an integer if necessary, and checked against the array's declared upper and lower bounds. If it is not in the allowable range, execution will terminate. For example, consider the code

```
200    DIM SCORES(25)
210    LET N = 15
220    LET SCORES(2*N) = 93
```

The subscript used in line 220 is 30, which is greater than the declared upper bound for the array SCORES (25). Thus, execution will halt at this point, and an error message similar to the following one will be displayed:

```
Subscript out of range in 220
```

Using One-Dimensional Arrays

As the next example demonstrates, counter-controlled loops are valuable tools in the manipulation of arrays. The loop counter keeps track of the array element being processed.

EXAMPLE 6.2   This program reads a set of 12 monthly rainfall figures, computes their average, and displays all this data.

```
100 REM     *****    AVERAGE MONTHLY RAINFALL    *****
110 REM              S. VENIT       JULY, 1987
120 REM
130 REM     THIS PROGRAM COMPUTES THE AVERAGE OF 12 MONTHLY
140 REM       RAINFALL FIGURES INPUT FROM DATA STATEMENTS
150 REM
160 REM     VARIABLES USED:
170 REM        RAIN() ..... THE ARRAY OF RAINFALL FIGURES
180 REM        SUM ........ THEIR SUM
190 REM        AVG ........ THEIR AVERAGE
200 REM
210         DIM RAIN(12)
220 REM
230         CLS
240         PRINT TAB(15); "MONTHLY RAINFALL FOR THE YEAR"
250         PRINT
260 REM
270         LET SUM = 0
280         FOR K = 1 TO 12
290            READ RAIN(K)
300            LET SUM = SUM + RAIN(K)
310         NEXT K
320 REM
330         LET AVG = SUM / 12
340 REM
350         PRINT "MONTH: ";
360         FOR K = 1 TO 12
370            PRINT USING "#####"; K;
380         NEXT K
390 REM
400         PRINT
410         PRINT "RAINFALL:";
420         FOR K = 1 TO 12
430            PRINT USING "##.##"; RAIN(K);
440         NEXT K
450 REM
460         PRINT
470         PRINT
480         PRINT "THE AVERAGE RAINFALL FOR THESE MONTHS IS: ";
490         PRINT USING "##.##"; AVG
500 REM
510         DATA 4.32, 4.67, 4.10, 3.42, 3.05, 2.54
520         DATA 2.10, 2.05, 2.78, 3.40, 3.87, 4.15
530 REM
540         END
```

In this program, the FOR/NEXT loops read, sum, and print all the elements in our array, RAIN. In other respects, this program would be similar to one that used 12 simple variables to accomplish the same task. The output is

```
          MONTHLY RAINFALL FOR THE YEAR
MONTH:     1    2    3    4    5    6    7    8    9   10   11   12
RAINFALL: 4.32 4.67 4.10 3.42 3.05 2.54 2.10 2.05 2.78 3.40 3.87 4.15

THE AVERAGE RAINFALL FOR THESE MONTHS IS:   3.37
```

The next example demonstrates the use of *parallel* arrays, ones in which elements with the same subscript are related.

EXAMPLE 6.3 This program segment inputs the names of salespersons and their total sales for the month into two parallel arrays and determines which salesperson has the best sales record.

```
200       DIM N$(100), SALES(100)
210 REM
220       LET MAX = 0
230       LET K = 1
240       INPUT "ENTER NAME AND MONTHLY SALES ", N$(K), SALES(K)
250 REM
260       WHILE N$(K) <> "*"
270          IF SALES(K) <= MAX THEN 300
280             LET INDEX = K
290             LET MAX = SALES(K)
300 REM      END IF
310          LET K = K + 1
320          PRINT "ENTER NAME AND SALES (ENTER  *,0  TO QUIT)"
330          INPUT N$(K), SALES(K)
340       WEND
350 REM
360       PRINT "MAXIMUM SALES FOR THE MONTH: "; SALES(INDEX)
370       PRINT "SALESPERSON:                "; N$(INDEX)
```

In this program segment, we do not use a FOR/NEXT loop to input the data because the number of salespersons may vary from run to run. We do, however, still need a counter to serve as a subscript for the array element currently being processed.

The determination of the maximum sales is done by the If Then structure in lines 270–300. When a "new" maximum sales figure is found, the array element at which this occurs (INDEX) is recorded and MAX is set equal to this new maximum value. After looping through all salespersons, we print the largest sales figure and the name of the salesperson who achieved it.

6.2 SORTING ARRAYS

Sorting data, that is, arranging it in some prescribed order, is one of the most common of programming tasks. For numbers, the prescribed order would be either *ascending* (from smallest to largest) or *descending* (from largest to smallest);

for strings it would usually be alphabetical. In this section we will discuss the **bubble sort** technique for sorting data.

To apply the bubble sort technique, we make several sweeps, or passes, through the data; on each pass we compare all adjacent pairs of data items and interchange (or swap) them if they are not already in the proper order. We continue making passes until no interchanges are necessary, which indicates that the data are now sorted.

To illustrate the bubble sort, let us first do a simple example by hand. Figure 6.2 demonstrates the process for a data set consisting of the numbers 9, 13, 5, 8, and 6. In each pass, we show the data at the start of the pass on the left and the results of the four comparisons in the next four columns. If an interchange takes place, the arrows cross, indicating which items have been swapped.

The bubble sort gets its name from the fact that, as we can see in figure 6.2, the larger numbers "sink" to the bottom of the list and the smaller ones "bubble" to the top. After the first pass, the largest number will be at the bottom (the end) of the list; after the second pass, the second largest will be next to last; and so on. Thus, in sorting N items, it will take *at most* N − 1 passes through the list to sort them (and one additional pass to determine that they are sorted).

The bubble sort of an array A of N numbers in ascending order is described in pseudocode as follows:

```
Do While array A is not sorted
    For K = 1, 2, . . . , N − 1
        If A(K) > A(K + 1) Then
            Interchange A(K) and A(K + 1)
        End If
    End For
End While
```

Before we can translate this pseudocode into BASIC, we must resolve two problems:

1. How to interchange two elements of an array

2. How to determine when no interchanges have taken place on a given pass

To interchange array elements A(K) and A(K + 1), we must temporarily store one of them in another location, call it TEMP, and then swap like this:

```
350    LET TEMP = A(K)
360    LET A(K) = A(K+1)
370    LET A(K+1) = TEMP
```

NOTE   In Microsoft BASIC, a single SWAP statement performs the same task as the three statements just shown. In Microsoft BASIC, lines 350–370 can be replaced by

```
350    SWAP A(K), A(K+1)
```

FIGURE 6.2

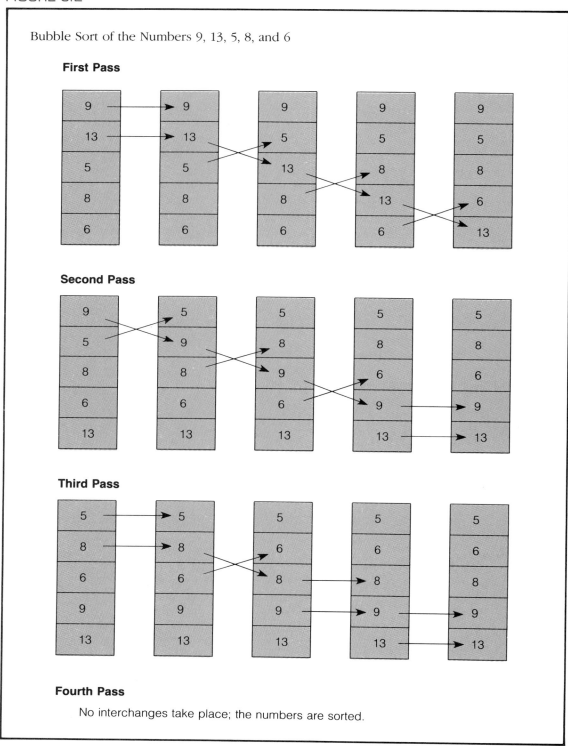

Bubble Sort of the Numbers 9, 13, 5, 8, and 6

First Pass

Second Pass

Third Pass

Fourth Pass

No interchanges take place; the numbers are sorted.

The SWAP statement

Form   SWAP variable1, variable2

Action   Interchanges the values of variable1 and variable2.

Examples
```
300     SWAP A$, B$
350     SWAP SALES(J), SALES(J+1)
```

We determine when to stop sorting by using a program flag. A **flag** (or **switch**) is a variable that takes on only two values during program execution, usually 0 and 1. When the flag is *set* (equal to 1), it typically indicates that a task has been accomplished; when it's *clear* (equal to 0), there is still work to be done.

In the bubble sort, a flag value of 0 will indicate that the list is still unsorted. We therefore initialize the flag to 0, and continue to reenter the Do While loop as long as the flag remains 0. Once inside the loop, we set it equal to 1 and only change it back to 0 if an interchange takes place. If no interchange occurs (meaning the data are sorted), the flag remains 1 and the loop is exited.

The next example provides the code for a typical bubble sort.

EXAMPLE 6.4   This program inputs a list of numbers and sorts it in ascending order by the bubble sort method.

```
100 REM   *****   BUBBLE SORT   *****
110 REM   S. VENIT          JULY, 1987
120 REM
130 REM   THIS PROGRAM SORTS THE NUMBERS INPUT IN
140 REM   ASCENDING ORDER BY THE BUBBLE SORT METHOD
150 REM
160 REM   VARIABLES:
170 REM      A() .... ARRAY TO BE SORTED
180 REM      FLAG ... 1 IF ARRAY IS SORTED, 0 OTHERWISE
190 REM      N ...... NUMBER OF ITEMS INPUT
200 REM
210       DIM A(100)
220 REM
230       CLS
240       PRINT "     ASCENDING SORT ROUTINE"
250       PRINT
260 REM
270 REM   INPUT NUMBERS TO BE SORTED
280 REM
290       LET N = 0
300       PRINT "TYPE NUMBERS TO BE SORTED PRESSING ENTER"
310       PRINT "AFTER EACH ONE.  ENTER -9999 WHEN DONE."
320       INPUT X
330 REM
340       WHILE X <> -9999
350          LET N = N + 1
360          LET A(N) = X
370          INPUT X
380       WEND
390 REM
400       PRINT
```

```
410        PRINT "       UNSORTED LIST ... "
420        FOR K = 1 TO N
430           PRINT A(K);
440        NEXT
450 REM
460 REM    SORT NUMBERS INPUT
470 REM
480        LET FLAG = 0
490        WHILE FLAG = 0
500           LET FLAG = 1
510           FOR K = 1 TO N - 1
520              IF A(K) <= A(K+1) THEN 570
530                 LET TEMP = A(K)
540                 LET A(K) = A(K+1)                    [SWAP A(K),A(K+1)]
550                 LET A(K+1) = TEMP
560                 LET FLAG = 0
570 REM          END IF
580           NEXT K
590        WEND
600 REM
610        PRINT
620        PRINT "       SORTED LIST ..."
630        FOR K = 1 TO N
640           PRINT A(K);
650        NEXT K
660 REM
670        END
```

A typical run of this program looks like this:

```
        ASCENDING SORT ROUTINE

TYPE NUMBERS TO BE SORTED PRESSING ENTER
AFTER EACH ONE.   ENTER  -9999  WHEN DONE.
? 9
? 13
? 5
? 8
? 6
? -9999

        UNSORTED LIST ...
  9   13   5   8   6
        SORTED LIST ...
  5   6   8   9   13
```

NOTE   We can use the code of example 6.4 to sort names into alphabetical order by just changing the array name from A to A$ wherever it appears. (In this case, lines 530–560 will be executed if—and only if—the name stored in A$(K+1) precedes, using alphabetical order, the one stored in A$(K).) Also, we can use virtually the same code as in example 6.4 to sort numbers in *descending* order; the only modification needed would be to change line 520 to read

```
520        IF A(K) >= A(K+1)   THEN 570
```

6.3   TABLE LOOKUP: SEARCHING AN ARRAY

Information arranged in tabular form (that is, as a table) is very common in business and mathematical applications as well as in everyday life. Some examples are bus schedules, baseball standings, student grade reports, and income tax tables. In this section, we will discuss a general way of searching a table for a particular entry. This procedure is called **table lookup.**

Suppose you have just arrived at the airport to meet an incoming passenger. You know her flight number but not the arrival time or gate, so you consult the posted flight information, given in the following tabular form:

ARRIVALS

Flight Number	Origin	Time	Gate
43	Kansas City	4:15	5
21	St. Louis	5:05	4
35	Dubuque	5:30	7
.	.	.	.
.	.	.	.
.	.	.	.

To find the arrival time and gate of your friend's flight, you scan down the leftmost column of this table until you locate her flight number and then move across that row to read the corresponding time and gate in the last two columns.

In going through this process, you have performed what is known as a table lookup. In data processing terminology, the item you were seeking (your friend's flight number) is called the **search key,** the list of all such items makes up the **table keys,** and the other data in the table are called the *table function values.* The way in which you looked for the desired flight number, checking them in the order listed, makes this a **serial search.**

In writing a program to do a table lookup, we have to

1. *Load the table.* Input the table (from DATA statements or external files, as in chapter 8) into arrays, one for each column of the table.

2. *Search the array that contains the table keys.* The search key is compared to the elements of this array, one by one, until a match occurs (or the end of the array is reached).

3. *Print the search key and corresponding table function values.* If the search key was not found in the array, print a message instead.

If the list of table keys is contained in an array A with N elements, the pseudo-code for performing a serial search for an item KEY is as follows:

Set the subscript of the table key sought (INDEX) to 0
Set FLAG = 0   [FLAG is set = 1 when KEY is found]

```
Do While FLAG = 0 and INDEX < N
    Increment INDEX by 1
    If A(INDEX) = KEY Then Set FLAG = 1
End While
```

Upon exit from the Do While loop, a FLAG value of 1 indicates that the search was successful—KEY has been found among the table keys—and INDEX gives its location (subscript) in the array A. If the value of FLAG is 0 upon loop exit, the search KEY was not found and we should print this fact.

The next example contains a table lookup done by a serial search technique.

EXAMPLE 6.5   This program loads a table containing student identification (ID) numbers, names, and placement test scores. It places this information into parallel arrays; performs a serial search for an ID number input by the user; and, if found, prints the corresponding name and test score.

```
100 REM      ******   SERIAL SEARCH   ******
110 REM      S. VENIT                JULY, 1987
120 REM
130 REM      THIS PROGRAM PERFORMS A SERIAL SEARCH FOR A KEY
140 REM      INPUT BY THE USER AND PRINTS THE CORRESPONDING
150 REM                   FUNCTION VALUES
160 REM
170 REM      VARIABLES:
180 REM          FLAG ...... SET = 1 IF KEY IS FOUND, 0 OTHERWISE
190 REM          ID() ...... ARRAY OF STUDENT ID NUMBERS
200 REM          INDEX ..... SUBSCRIPT OF TABLE KEY SOUGHT
210 REM          IDKEY ..... THE ID NUMBER SOUGHT
220 REM          N ......... NUMBER OF ITEMS IN EACH ARRAY
230 REM          SCORE() ... ARRAY OF STUDENT TEST SCORES
240 REM          STU$() .... ARRAY OF STUDENT NAMES
250 REM
260      DIM ID(1000), SCORE(1000), STU$(1000)
270 REM
280      CLS
290      PRINT "       STUDENT PLACEMENT TEST SCORES"
300      PRINT
310      PRINT "ENTER STUDENT ID NUMBER AND THE PROGRAM"
320      PRINT "WILL PRINT STUDENT NAME AND TEST SCORE."
330      INPUT IDKEY
340      PRINT
350 REM
360 REM      LOAD TABLE
370 REM
380      READ N
390      FOR K = 1 TO N
400          READ ID(K), STU$(K), SCORE(K)
410      NEXT K
420 REM
430 REM      PERFORM SERIAL SEARCH FOR KEY
440 REM
450      LET INDEX = 0
460      LET FLAG = 0
470 REM
480      WHILE INDEX < N AND FLAG = 0
490          LET INDEX = INDEX + 1
500          IF ID(INDEX) = IDKEY THEN LET FLAG = 1
510      WEND
```

```
520 REM
530 REM      PRINT STUDENT INFORMATION (OR 'NOT FOUND')
540 REM
550      IF FLAG = 1 THEN 580
560          PRINT "****    STUDENT ID NOT FOUND    ****"
570          GOTO 620
580 REM ELSE
590          PRINT "ID NUMBER ......"; IDKEY
600          PRINT "STUDENT NAME ... "; STU$(INDEX)
610          PRINT "TEST SCORE ....."; SCORE(INDEX)
620 REM END IF
630 REM
640      DATA 5
650      DATA 13576, W. BISHOP,       92
660      DATA 17215, R. JONES,        71
670      DATA 20345, A. GROSS,        89
680      DATA 21289, T. ROBINSON,     63
690      DATA 23416, E. PORTSMOUTH,   52
700 REM
710      END
```

Two runs of this program follow:

Run 1

```
        STUDENT PLACEMENT TEST SCORES

    ENTER STUDENT ID NUMBER AND THE PROGRAM
    WILL PRINT STUDENT NAME AND TEST SCORE.
    ? 23416

    ID NUMBER ...... 23416
    STUDENT NAME ... E. PORTSMOUTH
    TEST SCORE ..... 52
```

Run 2

```
        STUDENT PLACEMENT TEST SCORES

    ENTER STUDENT ID NUMBER AND THE PROGRAM
    WILL PRINT STUDENT NAME AND TEST SCORE.
    ? 11111

****     STUDENT ID NOT FOUND    ****
```

6.4 TWO-DIMENSIONAL ARRAYS

In the arrays you have seen so far, the value of an element (say, a student ID number or spare part name) has depended upon a single factor (in these cases, the student or part being processed). It is sometimes convenient to use arrays whose elements are determined by two factors, such as the score of a particular student on a particular test, or the sales of a certain salesperson in a certain month. In these cases, we use two-dimensional arrays.

Declaring Two-Dimensional Arrays

A **two-dimensional array** (sometimes called a **matrix**) is a collection of subscripted variables, each of which has two subscripts (separated by a comma). For example, A(2,3) is an element of a two-dimensional array named A. The next example illustrates one use of a two-dimensional array.

EXAMPLE 6.6   Suppose we want to input the test results for 30 students on five exams. We can use a single two-dimensional array named SCORES to hold all these test results. The first subscript of SCORES will reference a particular student; the second subscript, a particular test. For example, the array element SCORES(9,2) would contain the score of the ninth student on the second test.

This problem may be easier to understand if we picture the array elements in a rectangular pattern of horizontal rows and vertical columns. The first row gives all test scores of the first student; the second row, the scores of the second student; and so on. The first column gives the scores of all students on the first test; the second column, all scores on the second test; and so on. (See table 6.1.) The entry in the box at the intersection of a given row and column represents the value of that array element. For example, SCORES(2,4)—the score of Student 2 on Test 4—is 73 and SCORES(30,2)—the score of Student 30 on Test 2—is 76.

TABLE 6.1   AN ILLUSTRATION OF THE ARRAY SCORES FROM EXAMPLE 6.6

	Test 1	Test 2	Test 3	Test 4	Test 5
Student 1 →	92	94	87	83	90
Student 2 →	78	86	64	73	84
Student 3 →	72	68	77	91	79
.	.	.	.	.	.
.	.	.	.	.	.
.	.	.	.	.	.
Student 30 →	88	76	93	69	52

Like their one-dimensional counterparts, two-dimensional arrays should always be declared in a DIM statement before they are used. The array of example 6.6 can be dimensioned by the statement:

```
180    DIM SCORES(30,5)
```

The general form of this statement follows:

The DIM statement (general form)

Form   DIM var1(size1), var2(size2), ...
where var1, var2, ... are the array names, and size1, size2, ... represent either a single number or two numbers separated by a comma, and give upper bounds for the array subscripts

Action   Sets aside (allocates) storage locations in the computer's memory for the array elements.

Examples
```
150    DIM A(24,50)
160    DIM KIND$(10,10), SALES(12,8), SUM(100)
```

NOTES

1. *All* elements of a given array must be either numbers or strings; the two *cannot* be mixed in the same array.

2. We can mix one- and two-dimensional arrays in the same DIM statement. For example, the following statement is valid:

```
180    DIM A(10,20), B(5), C$(100)
```

3. The lower bound for all array subscripts will be either 0 or 1 depending upon your version of BASIC.

Using Two-Dimensional Arrays

As we have seen, counter-controlled loops, especially the FOR/NEXT variety, provide a valuable tool for manipulating one-dimensional arrays. For the two-dimensional kind, nested FOR/NEXT loops (see section 3.6) are especially useful.

EXAMPLE 6.7

This program segment reads data into a two-dimensional array and then prints it out in tabular form.

```
150      DIM SCORES(30,5)
160 REM
170 REM   READ FIVE TEST SCORES FOR THREE STUDENTS
180 REM
190      FOR ROW = 1 TO 3
200         FOR COL = 1 TO 5
210            READ SCORES(ROW,COL)
220         NEXT COL
230      NEXT ROW
240 REM
250 REM   PRINT THE STUDENT SCORES
```

```
260 REM
270       FOR ROW = 1 TO 3
280          FOR COL = 1 TO 5
290             PRINT SCORES(ROW,COL);
300          NEXT COL
310          PRINT
320       NEXT ROW
330 REM
340       DATA  92, 94, 87, 83, 90
350       DATA  78, 86, 64, 73, 84
360       DATA  72, 68, 77, 91, 79
```

In this program segment, the nested FOR/NEXT loops in lines 190–230 input numbers into the array SCORES. On the first pass through the outer loop, ROW = 1, so the five iterations of the inner loop read numbers into SCORES(1,1), SCORES(1,2), SCORES(1,3), SCORES(1,4), and SCORES(1,5). In other words, the first pass through the outer loop inputs all test results for the first student. On the next two passes, the scores for the other two students are read. (Notice that we have arranged the DATA statements as three rows of five numbers each. This is not necessary, but certainly increases the readability of the program.)

The nested output loops (lines 270–320) work in the same way to print the data in tabular form. (Statement 310 just moves the cursor from the end of one line to the beginning of the next.) The output produced is

```
92  94  87  83  90
78  86  64  73  84
72  68  77  91  79
```

NOTE   In example 6.7, an INPUT statement could be used instead of the READ to allow the user to enter the data. The input loop could be coded like this:

```
190       FOR ROW = 1 TO 3
200          PRINT "ENTER TEST SCORES FOR STUDENT"; ROW
205          PRINT "AFTER TYPING EACH SCORE, PRESS RETURN"
210          FOR COL = 1 TO 5
220             INPUT SCORE(ROW,COL)
230          NEXT COL
240          PRINT
250       NEXT ROW
```

REVIEW EXERCISES

Short Answer

1. How many storage locations will be allocated for the array A by each of the following? Assume that the smallest subscript is 0.

   a. 150   DIM A(12)

   b. 150   DIM A(5,10)

2. Answer the question posed in exercise 1, this time assuming that the smallest subscript is 1.

3. Determine whether each of the following statements is true or false.

    a. Arrays of string data and arrays of numeric data can be declared in the same DIM statement.

    b. All elements of an array must be of either string type or numeric type.

4. Determine whether each of the following statements is true or false.

    a. The bubble sort cannot be used to arrange numeric data in descending order.

    b. The serial search can only be used to locate a search key of numeric type.

Debugging

In exercises 5–8, the given program segments contain errors. Find and correct them.

5. Bubble sort of the array HOG in ascending order.

```
480        LET FLAG = 0
490        WHILE FLAG = 0
500           LET FLAG = 1
510           FOR K = 1 TO N - 1
520              IF HOG(K) <= HOG(K+1) THEN 560
530                 LET HOG(K) = HOG(K+1)
540                 LET HOG(K+1) = HOG(K)
550                 LET FLAG = 1
560 REM           END IF
570           NEXT K
580        WEND
```

6. Serial search of the array STAR for the element STARKEY.

```
450        LET INDEX = 0
460        LET FLAG = 0
470 REM
480        WHILE INDEX < N AND FLAG = 1
490           LET INDEX = INDEX + 1
500           IF STAR(INDEX) = STARKEY THEN LET FLAG = 0
510        WEND
```

7. The average of the elements of the array A.

```
600        LET SUM = 0
610 REM
620        FOR K = 1 TO N
630           LET SUM = SUM + A(K)
640        NEXT K
650 REM
660        LET AVG = SUM / K
```

8. The sum of the elements in each row of TEST.

```
700        FOR ROW = 1 TO M
710           FOR COL = 1 TO N
720              LET SUM(ROW) = 0
730              LET SUM(ROW) = SUM(ROW) + TEST(ROW,COL)
740           NEXT ROW
750        NEXT COL
```

Skill Builders

In exercises 9–11, what is displayed when each program segment is run?

9.
```
200   DIM X(100)
210   READ N
220   FOR K = 1 TO N
230      READ X(K)
240   NEXT K
260   PRINT X(1); X(N-1)
270   DATA  4, 3, 2, 1, 0
```

10.
```
300   DIM A$(20), B$(20)
310   FOR I = 1 TO 4
320      READ A$(I), B$(I)
330   NEXT I
340   FOR I = 1 TO 4
350      LET A$(I) = B$(5-I)
360      PRINT A$(I)
370   NEXT I
380   DATA  A,B,C,D,E,F,G,H
```

11.
```
400   DIM Q(10,10)
410   FOR R = 1 TO 3
420      FOR C = 1 TO 3
430         IF R = C THEN LET Q(R,C) = 1
440         IF R <> C THEN LET Q(R,C) = 0
450      NEXT C
460   NEXT R
470   FOR R = 1 TO 3
480      FOR C = 1 TO 3
490         PRINT Q(R,C);
500      NEXT C
510      PRINT
520   NEXT R
```

12. The following code is a modification of the bubble sort method for sorting an array A of N elements in ascending order:

```
900   FOR I = 1 TO N - 1
910      FOR J = I TO N - I
920         IF A(J) > A(J+1) THEN SWAP A(J), A(J+1)
930      NEXT J
940   NEXT I
```

a. If N = 4, how many comparisons will be made? (How many times will statement 920 be executed?)

b. Modify this program segment to sort A in descending order.

PROGRAMMING PROBLEMS

Write a BASIC program to solve each of the following problems:

1. Input a list of positive numbers, terminated by 0, into an array A. Then print the array and the largest and smallest number in it.

2. A *magic square* is a two-dimensional array of positive integers in which the number of rows equals the number of columns, and every row, every column, and the two diagonals add up to the same number. Input a two-dimensional array and determine if it is a magic square.

3. Input a list of employee names and salaries, and determine the mean (average) salary as well as the number of salaries above and below the mean.

4. The Eversoft Eraser Company has a list of their customers' names and addresses on DATA statements (terminated by *,*); this list contains some repeated entries. Print this mailing list in alphabetical order with no repeats.

5. The Department of Motor Vehicles of the state of Euphoria has finally decided to computerize its list of licensed drivers. The program should contain DATA statements each listing the name of a licensed driver, that driver's license number, and the number of outstanding warrants. The DATA statements should be arranged by license number in ascending order. (The last DATA statement should be a sentinel record with license number 0.) When a license number is input by the user, the corresponding name and number of warrants should be output by the program.

6. The Eversoft Eraser Company would like to have a program that prints a list of its inventory. This list will be entered into DATA statements of the form:

    ITEM NUMBER, ITEM NAME, PRICE, NUMBER IN STOCK

    The program should input the item number and quantity of erasers sold in the past day and print the revised inventory list. (Use a sentinel value to determine when all DATA have been read.)

7. The National Motor Company manufactures several (fewer than 10) automobile models. Its marketing director would like a program that inputs the names and annual sales figures of each model (both number sold and dollar amount) and determines its percentage of total sales. The program should also print the total number of cars sold as well as the company's total income from these sales.

8. The Finest Film Company has five different pay classifications for its hourly employees. Its payroll department would like to have a program to determine the gross weekly salary of these employees. The user would input the name, pay class, and hours worked for each employee. The program would print this information, as well as the employee's gross pay, all in table form. The hourly pay for the five classifications would be given in a DATA statement as:

    xxx   DATA 3.80, 4.20, 4.90, 6.10, 7.75

BASIC FUNCTIONS

A **function** is a subprogram that computes and returns a single value when called. It is termed a **numeric function** or a **string function** depending upon the type of value returned. In this chapter we will discuss the numeric and string functions that are supplied with most BASIC systems, as well as those that can be created by the programmer.

7.1   Built-in Numeric Functions

Built-in functions are those that are supplied with your BASIC system. The code for a built-in function does *not* appear in the program. It is inserted by the computer when the program is translated into machine language.

Arithmetic Functions

Table 7.1 lists some of the built-in numeric functions common to most versions of BASIC.

TABLE 7.1   ARITHMETIC FUNCTIONS

FUNCTION	ACTION	EXAMPLES
		(Where a variable is given, N = 3.6 and M = 9.)
`ABS(X)`	Returns the absolute value (the magnitude) of X.	`ABS(N) = 3.6` `ABS(-6.2) = 6.2`
`FIX(X)`	Truncates X and returns the integer part.	`FIX(N+1) = 4` `FIX(-N) = -3`
`INT(X)`	Returns the greatest integer less than or equal to X.	`INT(N+1) = 4` `INT(-N) = -4`
`SGN(X)`	Returns -1 if X $<$ 0, 0 if X = 0, or 1 if X $>$ 0.	`SGN(M) = 1` `SGN(-7.1) = -1`
`SQR(X)`	Returns the square root of a nonnegative number X.	`SQR(M) = 3` `SQR(M-5) = 2`

NOTE

In table 7.1, X represents the **argument** of the function. It can be a numeric constant, variable, or expression. A built-in numeric function is called by using it anywhere you would use a numeric constant. When a function is called, its argument must have already been assigned a value.

The INT function has several applications in BASIC programming. One of these is rounding. To round a positive number to the nearest integer, we add 0.5 to it and then truncate the decimal part. In general, we can round a positive number X to P decimal places by using the statement:

```
LET X = INT(X * 10^P + 0.5) / 10^P
```

EXAMPLE 7.1

This program segment reads a number from a DATA statement and displays its value rounded to the nearest integer, tenth, and hundredth.

```
200       READ NUM
210 REM
220       LET X = INT(NUM + 0.5)
230       LET Y = INT(NUM * 10 + 0.5) / 10
240       LET Z = INT(NUM * 100 + 0.5) / 100
250 REM
260       PRINT "THE NUMBER IS .........."; NUM
270       PRINT "TO NEAREST INTEGER ....."; X
280       PRINT "TO NEAREST TENTH ......."; Y
290       PRINT "TO NEAREST HUNDREDTH ..."; Z
300 REM
310       DATA 2.716
```

The output of this program segment is

```
THE NUMBER IS .......... 2.716
TO NEAREST INTEGER ..... 3
```

```
TO NEAREST TENTH ....... 2.7
TO NEAREST HUNDREDTH ... 2.72
```

The functions FIX(X) and INT(X) are identical if $X \geq 0$. When $X < 0$, they return the same number if X is an integer, but the value of INT is one less than that of FIX otherwise. For example, FIX(-3.7) = -3, but INT(-3.7) = -4. (The FIX function is not available on Apple II or Commodore 64 computers.)

In example 7.1, we used the INT function to round *positive* numbers. The FIX and SGN functions can be combined to round *any* number X to P decimal places by using the statement

```
LET X = FIX(X * 10 ^ P + SGN(X) * 0.5) / 10 ^ P
```

STYLE POINTER   Use Built-in Functions

You should always use the functions supplied by your BASIC system rather than writing the code to implement them yourself. Using these functions has the following advantages:

1. It will save you the time it takes to write the code.

2. The code for built-in functions is written in machine language and will be more efficient than your BASIC code.

3. It will result in a more readable program.

Exponential, Logarithmic, and Trigonometric Functions

Table 7.2 presents additional, more advanced mathematical functions common to most versions of BASIC.

TABLE 7.2   EXPONENTIAL, LOGARITHMIC, AND TRIGONOMETRIC FUNCTIONS

FUNCTION	ACTION	EXAMPLES
		(Where A = 1 and PI has the value π, approximately 3.1416)
EXP(X)	Returns e to the X power, where e ($= 2.71 \ldots$) is the base of the natural logarithm.	EXP(0) = 1
LOG(X)	Returns the natural (base e) logarithm of X.	LOG(A) = 0
COS(X)	Returns the cosine of X, where X is in radians.	COS(A − 1) = 1
SIN(X)	Returns the sine of X, where X is in radians.	SIN(PI/6) = .5
TAN(X)	Returns the tangent of X, where X is in radians.	TAN(PI/4) = 1
ATN(X)	Returns the arctangent (inverse tangent) of X	ATN(0) = 0

In all functions here, X represents a numeric expression.

Whenever you use one of the BASIC functions COS, SIN, or TAN, remember that its argument (the given angle) must be expressed in *radians*. (One radian is approximately 57 degrees.) If an angle is given in degrees, to convert it to radians, multiply by $\pi/180$, taking π to be 3.1416. For example, an angle of 30 degrees is approximately (3.1416/180) (30) = 0.52 radians. The next example illustrates this conversion in printing a table of the functions SIN, COS, and TAN.

EXAMPLE 7.2 This program segment prints the sine, cosine and tangent of angles from M degrees to N degrees, where M and N are read from a DATA statement.

```
380      READ M, N
390 REM
400 REM    PRINT TABLE HEADINGS
410 REM
420      PRINT TAB(5) "TABLE OF TRIGONOMETRIC FUNCTIONS"
430      PRINT
440      PRINT "X (DEG)      SIN(X)      COS(X)      TAN(X)
450      PRINT "------------------------------------------------"
460 REM
470 REM    PRINT TABLE ENTRIES
480 REM
490      LET C = 3.1416 / 180
500 REM
510      FOR ANGLE = M TO N
520          LET X = C * ANGLE
530          PRINT " "; ANGLE; TAB(11);
540          PRINT INT(SIN(X) * 10^4 + .5) / 10^4; TAB(21);
550          PRINT INT(COS(X) * 10^4 + .5) / 10^4; TAB(31);
560          PRINT INT(TAN(X) * 10^4 + .5) / 10^4
570      NEXT ANGLE
580 REM
590      DATA   30, 35
```

We begin this program segment by reading the initial and final values of the angles (in degrees) from the DATA statement. Then, after printing the table headings and defining the degree/radian conversion factor (C, line 490), we enter the FOR/NEXT loop to compute and print the table entries. Notice that prior to displaying these values, we first convert the ANGLE from degrees into radians (line 520).

The output produced by this program is as follows:

```
       TABLE OF TRIGONOMETRIC FUNCTIONS

X (DEG)      SIN(X)      COS(X)      TAN(X)
--------------------------------------------
     30        .5          .866        .5774
     31        .515        .8572       .6009
     32        .5299       .848        .6249
     33        .5446       .8387       .6494
     34        .5592       .829        .6745
     35        .5736       .8192       .7002
```

7.2 RANDOM NUMBERS

Random numbers, those whose values form an unpredictable sequence, have many applications in programming. One of their major uses is to provide an element of chance in computer games. They also have important, more serious uses such as simulating certain situations or processes in business, mathematics, engineering, and other disciplines. In this section, you will learn how to generate and use random numbers in your BASIC programs.

The RND Function

In BASIC, random numbers are generated by the RND function. This function returns an unpredictable real number that is greater than or equal to 0 and less than 1. For example, the code

```
200     FOR K = 1 TO 5
210        PRINT RND;
220     NEXT K
```

displays the five numbers:

```
.7151002   .683111   .4821425   .9992938   .6465093
```

The RND function

Form   RND

Action   Returns a random number lying between 0 and 1 (including 0, but not 1).

Example   `300  PRINT RND`

Note: To produce random numbers on the Apple II, we use RND(1); on the Commodore 64, RND(− 1).

We often want to generate random numbers that lie in some range other than 0 to 1. To do this, we transform the numbers produced by RND. For example, to generate random numbers that range from 0 to 5, we use the expression 5 ∗ RND, which "stretches" the range of RND by a factor of 5. To obtain random numbers in the range 1 to 10, we use 9 ∗ RND + 1. Here, the multiplier 9 stretches the range to run from 0 to 9, and the added 1 "shifts" it to run from 1 to 10.

In some applications, a range of random *integers* is needed. (The expressions given so far all result in *real* random numbers.) Random integers can be produced by using the INT function together with RND. For example, to generate a random integer from 1 to 6, we use INT(6 ∗ RND) + 1; its possible values are 1, 2, 3, 4, 5, and 6. (The multiplier 6 gives the number of integers in the range; the added 1 gives the value of the first of these integers.)

Table 7.3 summarizes this discussion and provides some examples.

TABLE 7.3   GENERATING RANDOM NUMBERS

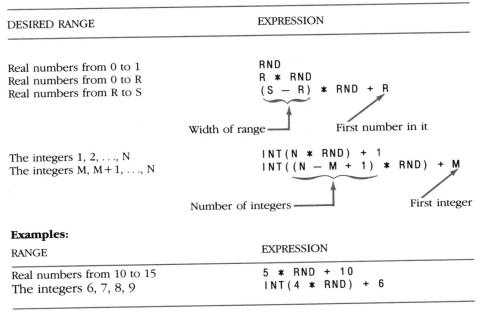

DESIRED RANGE	EXPRESSION
Real numbers from 0 to 1	RND
Real numbers from 0 to R	R * RND
Real numbers from R to S	(S — R) * RND + R

Width of range ——— First number in it

| The integers 1, 2, . . ., N | INT(N * RND) + 1 |
| The integers M, M+1, . . ., N | INT((N — M + 1) * RND) + M |

Number of integers ——— First integer

Examples:

RANGE	EXPRESSION
Real numbers from 10 to 15	5 * RND + 10
The integers 6, 7, 8, 9	INT(4 * RND) + 6

The RANDOMIZE Statement

The numbers returned by the RND function are produced by means of a mathematical algorithm. Given a starting number, called the **seed,** this algorithm generates a sequence of numbers which are random in the sense that any number between 0 and 1 is equally likely to occur. However, by virtue of the fact that the numbers are produced by an algorithm, they are not really unpredictable. (Such numbers are often called *pseudorandom.*) Nevertheless, for all practical purposes, the numbers generated by RND are as useful as those that are truly random.

When a program containing RND is run, the computer (unless instructed otherwise) always uses the *same seed* to generate its random numbers. This means that (except on the Apple II and Commodore 64 computers) the same sequence of random numbers will be produced each time a program is executed. Although this is useful for debugging purposes, once a program is functioning correctly we need to cause the computer to use a different seed on each run so that the random numbers produced will indeed be unpredictable.

We can choose a new seed by using the RANDOMIZE statement. The value of the expression following the keyword RANDOMIZE, rounded to the nearest integer if necessary, provides the value of the seed. For example, the statement

200   RANDOMIZE 100

sets the seed equal to 100. To obtain a different seed each time a program is executed, we can use the statement

```
300    RANDOMIZE VAL(RIGHT$(TIME$,2))
```

Statement 300 sets the seed equal to the number of seconds currently displayed on the computer's internal clock. (The TIME$ function reports the current time as an eight-character string of the form "hh:mm:ss", the RIGHT$ function returns the last two characters of this string, and the VAL function transforms them into a number. See sections 7.3 and 7.4.)

NOTE

Statement 300 will execute correctly in Microsoft BASIC (on the IBM PC, Apple Macintosh, and other computers). In some versions of Microsoft BASIC, we can obtain a similar effect by replacing line 300 with

```
300    RANDOMIZE TIMER
```

To obtain the effect of statement 300 in other dialects, change the original code as shown for each of the following computers:

Apple II	Delete the RANDOMIZE statement and replace RND by RND(1).
Commodore 64	Delete the RANDOMIZE statement and replace RND by RND(−1).
TRS-80	Replace the keyword RANDOMIZE by RANDOM.
VAX-11	Delete the expression VAL(RIGHT$(TIME$,2)) after the keyword RANDOMIZE.

The RANDOMIZE statement

Form RANDOMIZE numeric expression

Action Seeds the random number generator with the value of the numeric expression.

Example 300   RANDOMIZE VAL(RIGHT$(TIME$,2))

PROGRAMMING POINTER

The RANDOMIZE statement must be executed before the first use of the RND function. This can be assured by placing this statement at the beginning of the program (or program module).

The next example illustrates how random numbers can be used in programming simple games.

EXAMPLE 7.3   This program allows the user (presumably a small child) to play a guessing game with the computer.

```
100 REM    ************   OVER OR UNDER   ************
110 REM          S. VENIT      SEPTEMBER, 1987
120 REM
130 REM    THIS PROGRAM ALLOWS THE USER TO PLAY A GUESSING GAME
140 REM                    WITH THE COMPUTER
150 REM
160 REM    VARIABLES:
170 REM        GIVEN ... THE RANDOM NUMBER TO BE GUESSED
180 REM        GUESS ... THE USER'S GUESS
190 REM
200        RANDOMIZE VAL(RIGHT$(TIME$,2))
210        LET GIVEN = INT(100 * RND) + 1
220 REM
230        CLS
240        PRINT TAB(10); "THE OVER AND UNDER GAME"
250        PRINT
260        PRINT "I'M THINKING OF A NUMBER FROM 1 TO 100."
270        PRINT "   CAN YOU GUESS WHAT IT IS?"
280 REM
290 REM    CONTINUE UNTIL USER GUESSES THE NUMBER
300 REM
310        LET GUESS = GIVEN + 1
320        WHILE GUESS <> GIVEN
330            PRINT
340            INPUT "YOUR GUESS -----> ", GUESS
350            PRINT
360 REM
370 REM        COMPARE USER GUESS TO GIVEN NUMBER AND TAKE ACTION
380 REM
390            IF GUESS > GIVEN THEN PRINT "YOU'RE TOO HIGH!"
400            IF GUESS < GIVEN THEN PRINT "YOU'RE TOO LOW!"
410            IF GUESS = GIVEN THEN PRINT "CONGRATULATIONS! YOU WIN!!"
420 REM
430        WEND
440 REM
450        PRINT
460        PRINT "IT WAS FUN PLAYING WITH YOU.  GOODBYE FOR NOW."
470 REM
480        END
```

In this program, a random integer from 1 to 100 is generated by statement 210. Then the WHILE/WEND loop (lines 320–430) is executed repeatedly until the player guesses the secret number. To hasten this process, statements 390 and 400 state whether the guess is over or under the number sought. A typical run looks like this:

```
        THE OVER AND UNDER GAME

I'M THINKING OF A NUMBER FROM 1 TO 100.
        CAN YOU GUESS WHAT IT IS?

YOUR GUESS -----> 50

YOU'RE TOO LOW!
```

```
YOUR GUESS -----> 75
YOU'RE TOO LOW!
YOUR GUESS -----> 87
YOU'RE TOO HIGH!
YOUR GUESS -----> 82
CONGRATULATIONS! YOU WIN!!
IT WAS FUN PLAYING WITH YOU.  GOODBYE FOR NOW.
```

7.3 STRING FUNCTIONS; CONCATENATION

We have been using character strings (or more simply, strings) throughout the text in relatively simple ways. In this section, we will explore some of the more powerful ways in which we can use BASIC to manipulate strings. These include the processes of extracting substrings and combining two strings into a single new one.

Extracting Substrings

Any sequence of consecutive characters within a given string is called a **substring** of that string. For example, if TITLE$ = "THE SUN ALSO RISES", then "SUN", "SO R", and "T" are all substrings of TITLE$. On the other hand, "THIS" is not a substring; although the characters T, H, I, and S appear in TITLE$, they are not all adjacent to one another.

In processing text, we often have to extract substrings from a certain string: assign part of that string to its own variable. The string functions described in table 7.4 are useful for these purposes. **String functions,** unlike the *numeric* functions of section 7.1, either have a string argument or return a string value. (If an expression—a constant, variable, function, or any combination of these—has a string value, we call it a **string expression.)**

TABLE 7.4   THE LEFT\$, MID\$, RIGHT\$, AND LEN FUNCTIONS

FUNCTION	ACTION	EXAMPLES
		(Where T\$ = "ONE, IF BY LAND" and X = 3)
`LEFT$(A$,N)`	Returns the first N characters of A\$.	`LEFT$(T$,X) = "ONE"` `LEFT$(T$,X+4) = "ONE, IF"`
`MID$(A$,M,N)`	Returns the N character substring of A\$ beginning with the Mth character of A\$.	`MID$(T$,X,4) = "E, I"`
`MID$(A$,M)`	Returns the rightmost characters of A\$ beginning with the Mth one.	`MID$("CHATTER",2) = "HATTER"`
`RIGHT$(A$,N)`	Returns the last N characters of A\$.	`RIGHT$(T$,X) = "AND"` `RIGHT$("CHATTER",50) = "CHATTER"`
`LEN(A$)`	Returns the number of characters in A\$, its *length*.	`LEN(T$) = 15` `LEN(LEFT$(T$,3)) = 3`

In all cases here, A\$ is a string expression, and M and N are numeric expressions with nonnegative values, which are rounded to integers (if necessary).

NOTES   **1.** If a numeric argument (M or N in table 7.4) in LEFT\$, MID\$, or RIGHT\$ takes on a *negative* value, execution will terminate and an error message will be displayed.

2. If the value of N (the number of characters to be extracted in LEFT\$, MID\$, or RIGHT\$) has value 0, a **null string**—one that does not contain any characters—will be returned. This will also be the case if the value of M in MID\$ is greater than the length of A\$. For example,

`LEFT$("GREAT",0) = ""`   and   `MID$("GOOD",5,3) = ""`

Null string

3. On some time-sharing systems, RIGHT\$(A\$,M) returns the rightmost characters of A\$ beginning with the Mth one; that is, it acts like the function MID\$(A\$,M) described in table 7.4.

A string *function* can be used anywhere in a program that a string *constant* is valid. The next few examples illustrate the use of the string functions described in table 7.4.

EXAMPLE 7.4   This program segment inputs a date and outputs the month, day, and year.

```
200     PRINT "ENTER THE DATE IN THE FORM  MM/DD/YY"
210     PRINT "    FOR EXAMPLE,  05/17/78"
220     INPUT DT$
230     PRINT
240     PRINT "THE MONTH IS "; LEFT$(DT$,2)
250     PRINT "THE DAY IS "; MID$(DT$,4,2)
260     PRINT "THE YEAR IS 19"; RIGHT$(DT$,2)
```

A typical run of this program segment looks like this:

```
ENTER THE DATE IN THE FORM   MM/DD/YY
     FOR EXAMPLE,   05/17/78
? 12/15/79

THE MONTH IS 12
THE DAY IS 15
THE YEAR IS 1979
```

EXAMPLE 7.5 This program segment determines the number of words in the sentence input by counting the blanks and adding one. (We assume that the sentence is typed so that the only blanks in it are the single spaces between the words.)

```
300      PRINT "ENTER THE SENTENCE TO BE PROCESSED"
310      INPUT TEXT$
320      LET L = LEN(TEXT$)
330      LET COUNT = 1
340 REM
350      FOR K = 1 TO L
360         IF MID$(TEXT$,K,1) = " " THEN LET COUNT = COUNT + 1
370      NEXT K
380 REM
390      PRINT
400      PRINT "THE NUMBER OF WORDS IN:"
410      PRINT "     "; TEXT$
420      PRINT "IS"; COUNT
```

After the sentence is input, we find its length (line 320), which will be used as the limit value for our FOR/NEXT loop. We then initialize the COUNT to one (since the first word will not be preceded by a blank) and enter the loop. In each iteration, statement 360 inspects one character in the given sentence and increments COUNT whenever a blank is found. After all the characters in the sentence have been checked, the loop is exited and the results are printed. A typical run looks like this:

```
ENTER THE SENTENCE TO BE PROCESSED
? THE QUICK BROWN FOX JUMPED OVER THE LAZY DOG.

THE NUMBER OF WORDS IN:
    THE QUICK BROWN FOX JUMPED OVER THE LAZY DOG.
IS 9
```

The task of locating a substring within a given string is an important one and many versions of BASIC contain a string function, INSTR, that performs this operation. The INSTR function, which is illustrated in example 7.6, is described as follows:

The INSTR function

Form   INSTR(A$,B$)
            where A$ and B$ are string expressions

Action   Searches the string A$ for the substring B$ and returns the
            position of B$ if found; otherwise, it returns 0.

Examples INSTR("HI THERE","TH") = 4
            INSTR ("NOT HERE", "WHY") = 0

Note: This function is not available on the Apple II or Commodore 64 computers.

Concatenation

Arithmetic operators in BASIC, such as addition and multiplication, act on a pair of numbers to produce a numerical result. BASIC also provides a *string* operator, **concatenation,** which takes two strings and joins them together to produce a string result. The symbol used to concatenate two strings is the plus sign, +. For example, if A$ = "PART" and B$ = "TIME", then the statement

```
200   LET C$ = A$ + B$
```

assigns the string "PARTTIME" to the variable C$.
The next example illustrates an important use of the concatenation operator.

EXAMPLE 7.6   This program inserts a string input by the user into a given piece of text.

```
700        PRINT "THE TEXT IS:"
710        READ TEXT$
720        PRINT TEXT$
730 REM
740        INPUT "ENTER THE STRING TO BE INSERTED: ", I$
750        PRINT
760        PRINT "THIS STRING WILL BE INSERTED BEFORE THE"
770        INPUT "FIRST OCCURRENCE OF THE SUBSTRING ---> ", S$
780 REM
790        LET N = INSTR(TEXT$,S$)
800 REM
810        PRINT
820        IF N = 0 THEN 890
830           LET FIRST$ = LEFT$(TEXT$,N-1)
840           LET LAST$ = MID$(TEXT$,N)
850           LET NEWTEXT$ = FIRST$ + I$ + LAST$
860           PRINT "THE MODIFIED STRING IS:"
870           PRINT NEWTEXT$
880           GOTO 910
```

```
890 REM ELSE
900        PRINT "***    SUBSTRING NOT FOUND    ***"
910 REM END IF
920 REM
930     DATA  WE ARE NUMBER ONE!
```

To insert the input string (I$) into the text (TEXT$) before the specified substring (S$), we first have to locate the substring. This is done by statement 790, which either gives us the position (N) of S$ if it is found, or returns 0 if it is not. If S$ is found, the Then Clause (830–880) of the If Then Else structure breaks the given text into two parts (FIRST$ and LAST$) at the position of S$ (statements 830 and 840). It then reassembles the text, inserting I$ at the same time (statement 850), and prints the result.

The output of a typical run is

```
THE TEXT IS:
WE ARE NUMBER ONE!
ENTER THE STRING TO BE INSERTED: TWENTY-

THIS STRING WILL BE INSERTED BEFORE THE
FIRST OCCURRENCE OF THE SUBSTRING ---> ONE

THE MODIFIED STRING IS:
WE ARE NUMBER TWENTY-ONE!
```

7.4 THE ASCII CODE; MORE STRING FUNCTIONS

In this section, we will continue our discussion of character string processing. We will introduce the ASCII code, which sets up a correspondence between characters and numbers, and then discuss some built-in functions that convert data between string and numeric forms.

The ASCII Code

Since *all* data, including strings, are stored in the computer's memory as numbers (in binary form), every computer must have a scheme for associating a number with each character. On almost all computers this correspondence is given by the **ASCII** code (ASCII, pronounced "askey", stands for **A**merican **S**tandard **C**ode for **I**nformation **I**nterchange.)

Under this coding scheme, each character is associated with a number from 0 to 127. (Some computers have additional special characters with codes up to 255.) For example, the capital letters have ASCII codes from 65 ("A") to 90 ("Z"), the digits have codes from 48 ("0") to 57 ("9"), and the ASCII code for the blank is 32. Table 7.5 lists the ASCII codes for all *printable* characters; codes 0–31 represent *actions*, such as sounding a bell or beep (ASCII 7) or issuing a carriage return (ASCII 13), and are not shown in the table.

TABLE 7.5   THE ASCII CODES FROM 32 TO 127

CODE	CHARACTER	CODE	CHARACTER	CODE	CHARACTER
32	blank	64	@	96	`
33	!	65	A	97	a
34	"	66	B	98	b
35	#	67	C	99	c
36	$	68	D	100	d
37	%	69	E	101	e
38	&	70	F	102	f
39	'	71	G	103	g
40	(	72	H	104	h
41	)	73	I	105	i
42	*	74	J	106	j
43	+	75	K	107	k
44	,	76	L	108	l
45	—	77	M	109	m
46	.	78	N	110	n
47	/	79	O	111	o
48	0	80	P	112	p
49	1	81	Q	113	q
50	2	82	R	114	r
51	3	83	S	115	s
52	4	84	T	116	t
53	5	85	U	117	u
54	6	86	V	118	v
55	7	87	W	119	w
56	8	88	X	120	x
57	9	89	Y	121	y
58	:	90	Z	122	z
59	;	91	[	123	{
60	<	92	\	124	|
61	=	93	]	125	}
62	>	94	^	126	~
63	?	95	_	127	delete

The characters used in BASIC are ordered by the numerical order of their ASCII codes. For example, "*" < "3" because the ASCII codes for these characters are, respectively, 42 and 51. Similarly, "8" < "h" and "A" > " " (blank). Notice that

1. Letters are in alphabetical order.

2. Digits (viewed as characters) retain their natural order.

3. The blank precedes every other (printable) character.

The ASCII code also enables us to compare any two character strings. To determine which of two unequal strings comes first, use the following procedure:

Scan the strings from left to right, stopping at the first position for which the corresponding characters differ. Then, the ordering of these two characters determines the ordering of the given strings. If one string ends before any pair of corresponding characters differ, then the shorter string precedes the longer one.

EXAMPLE 7.7 Determine whether each of the following expressions is true or false.

> a. **"*?/!" < "*?,3"**   b. **"ANN" < "ANNE"**

For a.: The first pair of characters that differ occurs in the third position. Since "/" has code 47 and "," has code 44, the first string is greater than the second and therefore the expression is false.

For b.: The first string ends before any pair of characters differ. Hence, the first string is less than the second and the expression is true.

Converting between Characters and Their ASCII Codes

BASIC provides built-in functions that convert an ASCII code into the corresponding character and vice versa. Descriptions of these functions follow.

The ASC function

Form   ASC(C$)

Action   Returns the ASCII code corresponding to the character C$. (On some time-sharing systems, this function is ASCII(C$).)

Examples ASC("?") = 63
              ASC("R") = 82

Note: C$ represents a string expression of length one.

The CHR$ function

Form   CHR$(N)

Action   Returns the character corresponding to the ASCII code N.

Examples CHR$(58) = ":"
              CHR$(101) = "e"

Note: N represents a numeric expression (rounded to an integer, if necessary).

EXAMPLE 7.8   This program segment uses the CHR$ function to print the ASCII codes. Its output is shown in table 7.5.

```
200        PRINT "CODE        CHARACTER" TAB(25) "CODE        CHARACTER";
210        PRINT TAB(49) "CODE        CHARACTER"
220        PRINT
230 REM
240        FOR K = 32 TO 63
250            PRINT USING "###        \\"; K; CHR$(K);
260            PRINT TAB(25)
270            PRINT USING "###        \\"; K + 32; CHR$(K+32);
280            PRINT TAB(49)
290            PRINT USING "###        \\"; K + 64; CHR$(K+64)
300        NEXT K
310 REM
```

Converting between a Number and the Corresponding String

A number in BASIC can be treated as either numeric or string data. For example, the statement

```
500    LET X = 71
```

stores 71 as a number (in binary form). As numeric data, it can be manipulated by arithmetic operators ($+$, $-$, $*$, $/$, and $^$) and be used anywhere a numeric constant is permitted. On the other hand, the statement

```
600    LET X$ = "71"
```

stores the ASCII codes for 7 and 1, since "71" is a string. This form of the number 71 can be used anywhere a string constant is valid, but it cannot (for example) be multiplied or divided by a number.

Although we usually want to treat numbers as numeric data, it is sometimes useful to store them in string form. For example, if we want to display a number without a trailing blank, we could just print the corresponding string. To help us do these kinds of things, BASIC supplies built-in functions that convert numbers from numeric to string form and vice versa. Descriptions of these functions follow:

The STR$ function

Form   STR$(N)

Action   Returns the string equivalent of the number N.

Examples   STR$(71.5) = " 71.5"
                STR$(−53) = "−53"

The VAL function

Form   VAL(A$)

Action   Returns the numeric equivalent of the string A$, or 0 if the characters in A$ do not form a number.

Examples
```
VAL("89.43") = 89.43
VAL("TEXT") = 0
```

PROGRAMMING POINTER

In some forms of BASIC (including Microsoft) the STR$ function places a *leading blank* in the string equivalent of a positive number or 0. In such a dialect, to print a number X *without* a leading (or trailing) blank, we could use the code:

```
750      LET X$ = STR$(X)
760      IF X >= 0 THEN LET X$ = MID$(X$,2)
770      PRINT X$;
```

We say that the MID$ function in line 760 "strips off" the leading blank.

7.5   USER-DEFINED FUNCTIONS

BASIC also allows programmers to create their own functions. These are called **user-defined functions.** (Notice that here, the word *user* means the programmer, not the person who runs the program.) The code that creates this kind of function is given by a statement of the form

DEF FNname(arg, arg, . . .) = expression

where name is any valid (numeric or string) variable, arg represents a variable, and expression can be any numeric or string expression (as long as its type agrees with that of name). For example,

```
DEF FNAREA(R) = 3.1416 * R ^ 2
```

defines a function named AREA which computes the area of a circle of radius R.

NOTE   On the Apple II and Commodore 64 computers, the name of the function must be a single letter and only one argument is permitted. On the VAX-11 minicomputer, more general multiline functions can be defined.

To use a user-defined function, the DEF FN statement creating it must appear before the statement containing the function call. We call a user-defined function in the same way as a built-in function: by using it anywhere in the program that a constant of its type would be valid. In the function call, the function name must be immediately preceded by FN. The next example illustrates these points.

EXAMPLE 7.9   This program segment contains a user-defined function that rounds a number to any desired number of decimal places.

```
180     DEF FNROUND(N,P) = FIX(N * 10^P + SGN(N) * 0.5) / 10^P
190 REM
200     READ X, Y
210 REM
220     LET ROUNDX = FNROUND(X,1)
230     PRINT X; "ROUNDED TO THE NEAREST TENTH IS "; ROUNDX
240     LET ROUNDY = FNROUND(Y,2)
250     PRINT Y; "ROUNDED TO THE NEAREST HUNDREDTH IS "; ROUNDY
260 REM
270     DATA  -3.28, 5.375
```

The function ROUND is defined by statement 180 and called in lines 220 and 240. In the first call, the *parameters* N and P of the function definition are replaced by the values of X and 1, respectively, and the expression to the right of the equal sign is evaluated. This value is then assigned to ROUNDX. In the second call, N and P are replaced by the values of Y and 2, respectively, the expression evaluated, and the result assigned to ROUNDY. The output of this program segment is

```
-3.28 ROUNDED TO THE NEAREST TENTH IS -3.3
 5.375 ROUNDED TO THE NEAREST HUNDREDTH IS  5.38
```

PROGRAMMING POINTER

When calling user-defined functions that have several arguments, make sure that:

1. The *number* of arguments in the function call is the same as in the function definition.

2. The *order* in which the arguments appear in the function call is the same as in the function definition.

The DEF FN statement

Form   DEF FNname(arg, arg, ...) = expression
              where name is a variable name, arg (argument) is a
              variable, and expression is of the same type as name

Action   Defines the user-defined function *name*.

Examples   `DEF FNCUBE(X) = X^3`
              `DEF FNINVEST(P, R, T) = P * R * T`

REVIEW EXERCISES

Short Answer

1. If X = −3.25, what are the values of the following expressions?

    a. `ABS(X)`   b. `SGN(X)`   c. `FIX(X)`

2. If N = 2, what are the values of the following expressions?

    a. `SGN(SQR(N+1))` b. `ABS(INT(−N))` c. `FIX(N/5)`

3. What is the value of each of the following expressions?

    a. `INT(RND)`   b. `EXP(1)`   c. `EXP(LOG(1))`

4. Assume that the variable PI has the value π. What is the value of each of the
    following expressions?

    a. `SIN(PI/6)`   b. `COS(PI/3)`   c. `TAN(0)`

5. Determine which of the following expressions will generate a (real) random
    number in the range 2 through 5.

    a. `2 * RND + 5`   b. `2 * RND + 3`
    c. `3 * RND + 5`   d. `3 * RND + 2`

6. Which of the following expressions will generate a random integer in the
    range 1 through 10?

    a. `INT(10 * RND)`   b. `9 * RND + 1`
    c. `INT (9 * RND) + 1`   d. `INT(10 * RND) + 1`

In exercises 7–8, if A\$ = "TO ERR IS HUMAN", B\$ = "TO FORGIVE, DIVINE",
and X = 4, find the values of each function.

7. a. `LEFT$(A$,2)`   b. `MID$(A$,2,3)`
    c. `RIGHT$(B$,4)`   d. `LEN(B$)`

8. a. `INSTR(A$,"E")`   b. `INSTR(A$,"FOR")`
    c. `A$ + " " + B$`   d. `MID$(A$,X,3) + MID$(B$,X+1,2)`

In exercises 9–10, if F$ = "F", BLANK$ = " ", N = 3, and X = 37.1, find the value of each function.

9. a. `CHR$(49)`   b. `CHR$(10*N+5)`
    c. `ASC("Z")`   d. `ASC(F$)`

10. a. `STR$(3.5)`   b. `STR$(ASC(BLANK$))`
    c. `VAL("78.3")`   d. `VAL("X")`

In exercises 11 and 12, if J$ = "JOHN" and S$ = "SMITH", determine whether each of the following conditions is true or false.

11. a. `J$ < " JOHN"`   b. `J$ >= "JO"`   c. `J$ > "*JOHN*"`

12. a. `(J$ + " " + S$) < (S$ + ", " + J$)`
    b. `"**?" < "***"`
    c. `"** " < "***"`

13. Write a DEF FN statement that defines a function which

    a. rounds *any* number to two decimal places.
    b. finds the average of three numbers.
    c. finds the area of a triangle of given base and altitude.

Debugging

In exercises 14–18, correct the errors in each program segment.

14.
```
100 REM    THIS PROGRAM PRINTS THE SQUARE ROOT OF THE
110        SUM OF THE SQUARES OF THE TWO NUMBERS
120 REM
130        INPUT X, Y
140        DEF FNSUMSQ = A^2 + B^2
150        LET Z = SUMSQ(X, Y)
160        PRINT SQRT(Z)
170 REM
180        END
```

15.
```
600 REM    THIS CODE COMPUTES THE SIN AND COS OF THE ANGLE INPUT
610 REM
620        INPUT "ENTER AN ANGLE IN DEGREES", ANGLE
630        PRINT "THE SINE OF "; ANGLE; "IS "; SIN(ANGLE)
640        PRINT "THE COSINE OF "; ANGLE; "IS "; COS(ANGLE)
```

16.
```
700 REM     THIS CODE PRINTS 10 RANDOM INTEGERS IN THE
710 REM     RANGE FROM 1 TO 6
720 REM
730         FOR K = 1 TO 10
740             PRINT 6 * RND + 1
750             RANDOMIZE 100
760         NEXT K
```

17. The following program segment is supposed to count the number of words in the sentence input.

```
500         INPUT PHRASE$
510         LET K = 0
520 REM
530         FOR N = 1 TO LEN(PHRASE$)
540             IF MID$(PHRASE$,K,1) = " " THEN LET K = K + 1
550         NEXT N
```

18. The following program segment is supposed to print the word FOUND if the text input contains an asterisk.

```
600         INPUT PHRASE$
610         LET N = INSTR("*",PHRASE$)
620         IF N = 0 THEN PRINT "FOUND"
```

Skill Builders

In exercises 19 and 20, what is displayed when each program segment is executed?

19.
```
200         READ N$
210         PRINT LEFT$(N$,1);
220         LET N = INSTR(N$," ")
230         PRINT MID$(N$,N+1,1)
240         DATA    ALEC GUINNESS
```

20.
```
300         LET TEXT$ = "HE IS THERE"
310         LET L = LEN(TEXT$)
320         LET N = INSTR(TEXT$,"T")
330         PRINT LEFT$(TEXT$,N-1)
340         PRINT LEFT$(TEXT$,N-1) + RIGHT$(TEXT$,L-N)
350         PRINT LEFT$(TEXT$,N-1) + "W" + RIGHT$(TEXT$,L-N) + "?"
```

21. Create a user-defined string function that could be used to perform each of the following tasks:

a. Return the Kth character in the string TEXT$.

b. Return the initials of a person whose name N$ is listed in the form FIRST LAST.

22. Write a BASIC expression corresponding to each of the following mathematical expressions:

a. $\dfrac{e^x + e^{-x}}{2}$

b. $\cos^2 x + \sin^2 x$

PROGRAMMING PROBLEMS

Write a BASIC program to solve each of the following problems.

1. Print a table of values of EXP(X) and SQR(X) as X ranges from 1.0 to 2.0 in steps of 0.1. (The headings for this table should be X, EXP(X), and SQR(X).)

2. As a service to its customers, the Last National Bank wants to be able to compute how long it will take an investment to double in size at a given rate of interest. They need a program that will input the initial amount invested (P), the percentage rate of interest (R), and the frequency of compounding (N); and output the required term, T. This can be done by using the formula:

$$T = \frac{LOG(2)}{N * LOG(1 + S/N)}$$

where S = R / 100.

3. Input the lengths of the two shorter sides, *a* and *b*, of a right triangle and determine the hypotenuse, *c*, and the two acute angles, A and B.

   Hint: To compute the hypotenuse, use the *Pythagorean theorem*:

   $$c^2 = a^2 + b^2$$

   or

   $$c = \sqrt{a^2 + b^2}$$

   To compute the acute angles, use the ATN function and then the fact that A + B = 90 degrees.

4. a. Print an array of 25 different random numbers in the range 1 through 100.
   b. Print the array of part a. in ascending order.

5. A list of names is contained in DATA statements, the first of which gives the number, N, of names to follow. From this list, randomly select a first-, second-, and third-place prize winner. (*Hint:* Load the list into an array and then generate three random integers in the range 1 through N.) Test your program using the data:

```
5
G. BROCK
L. CARLTON
B. DOWNING
W. JOHNSON
W. WILSON
```

6. Input a line of text from the user and print the number of words and the number of vowels it contains.

7. Read several lines of text from DATA statements (terminated by three backslashes, \\\), replacing each occurrence of the letter *E* with an *, deleting each occurrence of the letter *S*, and printing the modified text.

8. A list of names is contained in DATA statements in the form FIRST LAST (terminated by "ZZZ"). Print a list of these names in the form LAST, FIRST sorted alphabetically by last name. Run your program using the data:

```
DATA HARRY TRUMAN
DATA DWIGHT EISENHOWER
DATA JOHN KENNEDY
DATA LYNDON JOHNSON
DATA ZZZ
```

DATA FILES

To enter data into our programs thus far, we have used LET, INPUT, and READ statements. In this chapter, we will discuss another way: using data files. A **data file** is a collection of related groups of data (the file **records**) stored on magnetic tape or disk separately from the program that uses it.

Using data files offers several significant advantages over other forms of input.

1. Data files can be used by more than one program.

2. Data files can store the *output* of a program for future review or as *input* for another program.

3. Data files can be created or modified by a program.

The data files we will discuss are **sequential files,** those in which the records must be processed in the order in which they were created. For example, to print the 50th record in a file, we must first "flip through" the 49 that precede it; we cannot access it directly.

8.1 CREATING A SEQUENTIAL FILE

To some extent, a sequential file resembles a series of DATA statements. Each record in a file (like each DATA statement) is terminated by a carriage return, and the items within it (its **fields**) are separated by commas. Moreover, to read a certain file record (or DATA statement), we must first read all those that precede it. However, whereas DATA statements are created by simply typing them at the keyboard, data files are set up by a program (or program segment) written expressly for this purpose.

The code to create a sequential file must contain:

1. An OPEN statement that names the file, declares its *mode* as OUTPUT, and assigns a *file number* to it.

2. A PRINT# (or WRITE#) statement that *writes* (transmits) the desired data to the file.

3. A CLOSE statement that disassociates the file from the file number and mode set up when it was opened.

Our first example illustrates this process.

EXAMPLE 8.1 This program segment creates a file called EMPLOYEE containing a list of names input by the user.

```
200      OPEN "EMPLOYEE" FOR OUTPUT AS #1
210 REM
220      LET NM$ = "AAA"
230      WHILE NM$ <> "ZZZ"
240         INPUT "ENTER EMPLOYEE NAME (OR 'ZZZ' WHEN DONE) ", NM$
250         PRINT #1, NM$
260      WEND
270 REM
280      CLOSE #1
```

In this program segment, the OPEN statement (line 200) assigns the number 1 to a file that will be referenced as EMPLOYEE, and prepares it for OUTPUT (to be created). Then, statement 220 initializes NM$ and ensures that the WHILE/WEND loop will be executed at least once. Within this loop, each name is input from the user, and then written to the file by the PRINT# statement (line 250). After entering the final name, the user types the sentinel value, ZZZ, which is also written to the file as an *end-of-file indicator*. (It will be a sentinel record for other programs using the file EMPLOYEE as input data.) Finally, the file is closed by statement 280.

Suppose the data entered by the user is

```
ENTER EMPLOYEE NAME (OR 'ZZZ' WHEN DONE)   DAVIS
ENTER EMPLOYEE NAME (OR 'ZZZ' WHEN DONE)   HANSON
ENTER EMPLOYEE NAME (OR 'ZZZ' WHEN DONE)   MARCUS
ENTER EMPLOYEE NAME (OR 'ZZZ' WHEN DONE)   ZZZ
```

Then, after execution of this program segment, the file EMPLOYEE is stored on disk, and can be pictured as:

```
DAVIS<CR>HANSON<CR>MARCUS<CR>ZZZ<CR><EOF>
```

where ⟨CR⟩ is a carriage return symbol and ⟨EOF⟩ is an end-of-file symbol placed there by the computer.

PROGRAMMING POINTER

If a file is opened for OUTPUT and a file of that name already exists on the disk, all data in the existing file will be lost. As we shall see, this is sometimes useful when modifying a file, but it may have catastrophic results if done accidentally.

The name of the file created in example 8.1 is EMPLOYEE. In general, *file names* in Microsoft BASIC (which is fairly typical) may consist of two parts separated by a period, as:

name.extension

where name is one to eight characters long (in some dialects only six characters are permitted), and the period and extension are optional. If the extension does appear, it may be one, two, or three characters long (see table 8.1). (Extensions are sometimes included to identify the *type* of file; for example, DAT for a data file, BAS for a BASIC file, and so on.)

TABLE 8.1   SOME VALID AND INVALID FILE NAMES

VALID	INVALID
PAYROLL	SALES 86 (blank not permitted)
PAYROLL.DAT	INVENTORY.DAT (name is too long)
GRADES.9A	COURSE.BASIC (extension is too long)

NOTE   If you want to write a file to a disk drive other than the current one, in the OPEN statement precede the file's name by the drive letter and a colon (:). For example, "B:INVLIST" refers to a file named INVLIST which will be created (or can be found) on the B (right-hand) drive.

In order to be easily retrieved, data items within a file record must be separated by commas placed there when the file is written. The next example demonstrates one way of doing this.

EXAMPLE 8.2   This program creates a file called GRADES containing records of the form

student name, test score

```
100 REM    ***********   GRADES CREATOR   ***********
110 REM           S. VENIT      OCTOBER, 1987
120 REM
130 REM    THIS PROGRAM CREATES A DATA FILE CALLED "GRADES"
140 REM
150 REM    FILE — "GRADES"
160 REM       STU$ ..... STUDENT NAME
170 REM       SCORE .... TEST SCORE
180 REM
190        OPEN "GRADES" FOR OUTPUT AS #1
200 REM
210        CLS
220        PRINT "THIS PROGRAM ALLOWS YOU TO ENTER THE NAMES"
230        PRINT "OF YOUR STUDENTS AND A TEST SCORE FOR EACH"
240        PRINT
250        PRINT "     ENTER STUDENT NAMES AND SCORES"
260        PRINT "        ENTER ZZZ, 0 WHEN DONE"
270        PRINT
```

```
280        LET STU$ = "AAA"
290 REM
300        WHILE STU$ <> "ZZZ"
310            INPUT "NAME, SCORE --------> ", STU$, SCORE
320            PRINT #1, STU$; ","; SCORE
330        WEND
340 REM
350        CLOSE #1
360        END
```

The PRINT# statement writes the same information to a file that the corresponding PRINT statement would display on the screen. For example, suppose the input on a run of this program is

```
NAME, SCORE --------> JONES, 86
NAME, SCORE --------> MARTIN, 73
NAME, SCORE --------> SMITH, 94
NAME, SCORE --------> ZZZ, 0
```

After execution, the file GRADES would contain the following data:

```
JONES, 86 <CR>MARTIN, 73 <CR>SMITH, 94 <CR>ZZZ, 0 <CR><EOF>
```

(Notice that PRINT# even places blanks before and after every positive number in the file, just as PRINT would do on the screen.)

STYLE POINTER Identify the Files Used in a Program

Data files, like variables and subroutines, should be listed in the header comments of the program module in which they are used. Both the file name and the variables used to represent the items within a record (its fields) should be listed and described (see example 8.2).

In using the PRINT# statement to write data to a file, it is bothersome to type ", " between each item in a record. In Microsoft BASIC, the WRITE# statement performs this function (and encloses each string written to the file in quotation marks as well). Thus, using WRITE# instead of PRINT#, line 320 of example 8.2 could be written more simply as:

```
320    WRITE #1, STU$, SCORE
```

After execution of the resulting program, the file would contain:

```
"JONES",86<CR>"MARTIN",73<CR>"SMITH",94<CR>"ZZZ",0<CR><EOF>
```

(Notice that WRITE# does not create blanks before or after numbers.)
    The OPEN, CLOSE, PRINT#, and WRITE# statements used in BASIC to create a sequential file are now summarized.

The OPEN statement

Form   OPEN "filename" FOR mode AS #filenumber
or
OPEN mode1, #filenumber, "filename"
where mode is INPUT or OUPTPUT; mode1 is "I" or "O";
and filenumber is either 1, 2, or 3
(Some versions of Microsoft BASIC require the second
form.)

Action   Names the file, states whether it will be read from or
written to, and assigns it a file number.

Examples

```
200    OPEN "FOO.DAT" FOR OUTPUT AS #2
220    OPEN "O", #1, "GRADES.101"
```

The CLOSE statement

Form   CLOSE #filenumber1, #filenumber2, . . .

Action   Terminates the mode of the listed files and frees their file
numbers for use by another file.

Example

```
600    CLOSE #1, #3
```

The PRINT# statement

Form   PRINT #filenumber, list of expressions
where list of expressions has the same form as the list for
a PRINT statement

Action   Writes data to the indicated file in the same form as it
would appear on the screen.

Examples

```
300    PRINT #1, A; ","; B$; ","; C
310    PRINT #3, NUM; ","; "KILROY WAS HERE"
```

The WRITE# statement

Form   WRITE #filenumber, list of expressions

Action   Same as PRINT# except that commas are written to the file between items in the list and strings are enclosed in quotation marks.

Example   400   WRITE #2, A, B, C$

8.2 READING A SEQUENTIAL FILE

Once a file has been created, we can input (or *read*) data contained within it into a program. The next example demonstrates how this is done.

EXAMPLE 8.3   This program segment displays the contents of the file GRADES created by the program in example 8.2.

```
200      OPEN "GRADES" FOR INPUT AS #1
210 REM
220      PRINT "STUDENT NAME", "TEST SCORE"
230      PRINT "------------", "----------"
240 REM
250      INPUT #1, STU$, SCORE
260      WHILE STU$ <> "ZZZ"
270          PRINT STU$, SCORE
280          INPUT #1, STU$, SCORE
290      WEND
300 REM
310      CLOSE #1
```

In this program segment, the OPEN statement opens the file GRADES for INPUT, allowing the transfer of data *from* the file *to* the program to take place. The INPUT# statements (lines 250 and 280) read a pair of data items from the file and assign them to the variables STU$ and SCORE. These values are then displayed on the screen by the PRINT statement in line 270. (It may be easier to understand the action of this program segment if you mentally replace the INPUT #1 by READ and picture the records in the file as a series of DATA statements.)

With the file GRADES as created in example 8.2, the output of this program will be

```
STUDENT NAME  TEST SCORE
------------  ----------
JONES             86
MARTIN            73
SMITH             94
```

PROGRAMMING POINTER

Before a file can be opened for INPUT, it must exist on your disk. It is permissible to create a file and read from it in the same program, but the file must be closed and reopened for INPUT between the two operations.

The general form of the INPUT# statement follows:

The INPUT# statement

Form   INPUT #filenumber, variable1, variable2, . . .

Action   Reads data items from the indicated file and assigns them to the listed variables.

Example   400   INPUT #3, EMP$, HOURS, RATE

The next example illustrates how to read and display *selected* information from a sequential file.

EXAMPLE 8.4   Suppose that a file named INVLIST contains an inventory of spare parts with records of the form

part number (PNUM), name (PNM$), price (PCST), quantity (PAMT)

terminated by the sentinel record 0,"*",0,0. The following program segment inputs a part number from the user and performs a serial search of the file for this number. If it is found, the information about that part is listed; otherwise, a NOT FOUND message is printed.

```
200       OPEN "INVLIST" FOR INPUT AS #2
210 REM
220       INPUT "ENTER PART NUMBER ----->", NUM
230       LET FOUND = 0
240       LET PNUM = 1
250 REM
260       WHILE PNUM <> 0 AND FOUND = 0
270          INPUT #2, PNUM, PNM$, PCST, PAMT
280          IF PNUM = NUM THEN LET FOUND = 1
290       WEND
300 REM
310       IF FOUND = 1 THEN 340
320          PRINT "PART"; NUM; "NOT FOUND"
330          GOTO 390
340 REM ELSE
350          PRINT "FOR PART"; NUM
360          PRINT "   NAME ........ "; PNM$
370          PRINT "   PRICE ....... "; PCST
```

```
380         PRINT "    QUANTITY ..... "; PAMT
390 REM END IF
400 REM
410      CLOSE #2
```

In Microsoft BASIC, we can test for the end of a file by using an *end-of-file* (EOF) function instead of a sentinel record; a description of this function follows:

The EOF function

Form   EOF(filenumber)

Action   Returns "true" (-1) if the last data item in the file has been processed (the EOF marker has been reached) and "false" (0) otherwise.

Example   500   IF EOF(3) THEN PRINT "WE ARE DONE"

EXAMPLE 8.5   If the file INVLIST in example 8.4 were created without the sentinel record, to achieve the same effect using an EOF function, we would:

1. Delete line 240 (we need not initialize PNUM).

2. Replace line 260 by

```
260    WHILE NOT EOF(2) AND FOUND = 0
```

8.3   MODIFYING A SEQUENTIAL FILE

In this section we will discuss how to make changes in an existing sequential file, a group of processes known collectively as **file maintenance.** These include adding records to, deleting records from, and modifying the data within a given data file.

Deleting, Adding, and Modifying Records

Sequential files cannot be modified quickly. If any change is made, the entire file must be *rewritten*. Every record in it must be read (and modified if so desired), temporarily stored somewhere else, and, after all records have been processed, written back to the given file.

One general procedure to accomplish this uses a second file, called a *scratch* file, to temporarily store the contents of the given file. The process proceeds as follows:

1. Open the given file for INPUT and the scratch file for OUTPUT.

2. Input data concerning the change from the user.

3. Read records from the given file and write them to the scratch file until you reach the one to be modified.

4. Make the change: write a new or modified record to the scratch file, or in the case of a deletion, do *not* write the specified record to the scratch file.

5. Read the rest of the records from the given file and write them to the scratch file.

6. Close both files.

7. Transfer all data from the scratch file to the given file.

The next few examples illustrate the maintenance process. In all of these, we assume that the file GRADES has been created as in example 8.2, with records of the form

> student name, test score

arranged in alphabetical order and terminated by "ZZZ", 0.

EXAMPLE 8.6   In this program segment, we create a file called SCRATCH which is identical to GRADES except for a record *deleted* at the request of the user.

```
200       OPEN "GRADES" FOR INPUT AS #1
210       OPEN "SCRATCH" FOR OUTPUT AS #2
220 REM
230       INPUT "NAME OF STUDENT TO BE DELETED"; NM$
240       LET STU$ = "AAA"
250 REM
260       WHILE STU$ <> "ZZZ"
270          INPUT #1, STU$, SCORE
280          IF STU$ <> NM$ THEN WRITE #2, STU$, SCORE
290       WEND
300 REM
310       CLOSE #1, #2
```

In this program segment, the WHILE/WEND loop reads all records, one at a time, from GRADES and writes each of these, *except* for the specified one, onto SCRATCH. At the end of execution, SCRATCH is identical to GRADES, except for the deleted record. For example, suppose GRADES contains

> "JONES",86<CR>"MARTIN",73<CR>"SMITH",94<CR>"ZZZ",0<CR><EOF>

and the user inputs the name MARTIN. Then, after execution, SCRATCH would contain

> "JONES",86<CR>"SMITH",94<CR>"ZZZ",0<CR><EOF>

The file GRADES will not change during the execution of the program segment in example 8.6. To restore GRADES as the name of the *updated* (modified) file, we could execute the following program segment:

```
320 REM
330     OPEN "GRADES" FOR OUTPUT AS #1
340     OPEN "SCRATCH" FOR INPUT AS #2
350     LET STU$ = "AAA"
360 REM
370     WHILE STU$ <> "ZZZ"
380         INPUT #2, STU$, SCORE
390         WRITE #1, STU$, SCORE
400     WEND
410 REM
420     CLOSE #1, #2
```

This code copies the file SCRATCH onto the file GRADES. (Remember: when GRADES is opened for OUTPUT in line 330, its contents are erased.)

However, this copying process is a very inefficient one. A much better way, available in most BASIC dialects, is to simply *rename* the scratch file as GRADES. To do this in Microsoft BASIC, we use the pair of statements:

```
320     KILL "GRADES"
330     NAME "SCRATCH" AS "GRADES"
```

The KILL statement erases the file GRADES (which has to be done before the renaming) and the NAME statement renames SCRATCH. (Both files must be closed prior to execution of these statements.) After the renaming, only one file, GRADES, will appear in the disk directory.

The general form of these statements follows:

The KILL and NAME statements

Form	KILL "filename" NAME "filename1" AS "filename2"
Action	KILL deletes filename from the disk; NAME renames filename1 as filename2.
Examples	`500     KILL "PAYROLL"` `510     NAME "FOO.DAT" AS "PAYROLL"`

EXAMPLE 8.7   This program segment *inserts* a record specified by the user into the GRADES file at the appropriate place (retaining alphabetical order).

```
200     OPEN "GRADES" FOR INPUT AS #1
210     OPEN "SCRATCH" FOR OUTPUT AS #2
220 REM
230     INPUT "NEW STUDENT AND SCORE"; NM$, SC
```

```
240 REM
250     WHILE NM$ > STU$
260         INPUT #1, STU$, SCORE
270         IF NM$ < STU$ THEN WRITE #2, NM$; SC
280         WRITE #2, STU$; SCORE
290     WEND
300 REM
310     WHILE STU$ <> "ZZZ"
320         INPUT #1, STU$, SCORE
330         WRITE #2, STU$; SCORE
340     WEND
350 REM
360     CLOSE #1, #2
370     KILL "GRADES"
380     NAME "SCRATCH" AS "GRADES"
```

The first WHILE/WEND loop (lines 250–290) reads records from the GRADES file and writes them onto the scratch file until the input name (NM$) precedes (in alphabetical order) the current record name (STU$). At this point, the new record is written to the scratch file, as well as the current record, and the loop is exited. The second WHILE/WEND loop (lines 310–340) reads the rest of the records from GRADES and writes them to SCRATCH. Finally, statements 370 and 380 rename the updated file as GRADES.

If prior to execution of this program segment, GRADES contains

```
"JONES",86<CR>"SMITH",94<CR>"ZZZ",0<CR><EOF>
```

and the user inputs the name POST and the score 71, then after execution, GRADES would contain the data

```
"JONES",86<CR>"POST",71<CR>"SMITH",94<CR>"ZZZ",0<CR><EOF>
```

EXAMPLE 8.8 This program segment *modifies* a specified record in GRADES in the way indicated by the user.

```
200     OPEN "GRADES" FOR INPUT AS #1
210     OPEN "SCRATCH" FOR OUTPUT AS #2
220 REM
230     INPUT "ENTER NAME OF STUDENT ----> ", NM$
240     INPUT "NEW TEST SCORE ----------> ", SC
250     LET STU$ = "AAA"
260 REM
270     WHILE STU$ <> "ZZZ"
280         INPUT #1, STU$, SCORE
290         IF STU$ = NM$ THEN WRITE #2, NM$, SC
                         ELSE WRITE #2, STU$, SCORE
300 REM     END IF
310     WEND
320 REM
330     KILL "GRADES"
340     NAME "SCRATCH" AS "GRADES"
```

Here, the WHILE/WEND loop copies all records from GRADES onto SCRATCH *except* for the one to be modified. It is replaced (due to the IF . . . THEN . . .ELSE statement) by the one containing the input data. Thus, if prior to execution, GRADES contains

```
"JONES",86<CR>"POST",71<CR>"SMITH",94<CR>"ZZZ",0<CR><EOF>
```

and the user enters the name SMITH and the score 96, then after execution, the GRADES file will contain

```
"JONES",86<CR>"POST",71<CR>"SMITH",96<CR>"ZZZ",0<CR><EOF>
```

REVIEW EXERCISES

Short Answer

In exercises 1–4, determine whether each of the statements is true or false.

1. a. A file can be used by more than one program.
   b. A file can store a program's output for future use.
   c. A file name cannot contain any blanks.

2. a. To read a given record in a sequential file, we must first read all those that precede it.
   b. If a file is opened for OUTPUT, and a file of that name already exists on the disk, then an error message is displayed.
   c. To be read by an INPUT# statement, data items in a file must be separated by commas or carriage returns.

3. a. A PRINT# statement writes the same characters to a sequential file as the corresponding PRINT statement would have displayed on the screen.
   b. When a file is opened for INPUT, data can be written from the program to the file.
   c. If a sequential file is created and then read in the same program, it must be closed and reopened between these operations.

4. a. If any change is made to a sequential file, the entire file must be rewritten.
   b. A file cannot be renamed with the name of another file that already exists on the disk unless the latter is first deleted.
   c. In order to delete a record from a file, we use the KILL statement.

Debugging

In exercises 5 and 6, correct the syntax errors in each statement.

5. a. 200   OPEN "FILE1" AS #1 FOR OUTPUT

```
b. 250    WRITE #2 A, B, C
c. 300    KILL FILE3
```

6. a. 200   NAME "MASTER" FOR "UPDATE"

   b. 250   INPUT #1, COST; PROFIT

   c. 300   PRINT #3 A$; ","; B

7. The following program segment is supposed to create and display (on the screen) a file containing the integers from 1 to 100, but it does not run properly. Correct the errors.

```
200       OPEN "WRONG" FOR INPUT AS #1
210       FOR K = 1 TO 100
220          PRINT #1, K
230       NEXT K
240       FOR K = 1 TO 100
250          INPUT #1, K
260          PRINT #2, K
270       NEXT K
280       CLOSE #1
```

8. The code in exercise 12 is supposed to insert the record "D", 90 into the proper place in the file ORIGINAL. Modify that program segment so that it does.

Skill Builders

In exercises 9 and 10, assume that a file SALES has been created by the following code:

```
200       OPEN "SALES" FOR OUTPUT AS #1
210       LET PERSON$ = "AAA"
220 REM
230       WHILE PERSON$ <> "ZZZ"
240          READ PERSON$, AMT
250          WRITE #1, PERSON$, AMT
260       WEND
270 REM
280       CLOSE #1
290       DATA  BURTON, 12360, LOCKE, 10580, POST, 14120, ZZZ, 0
```

What is displayed when each of the following program segments is run?

9. 200   OPEN "SALES" FOR INPUT AS #1
    210   LET NM$ = "AAA"
    220   WHILE NM$ <> "ZZZ"
    230   INPUT #1, NM$, TOT
    240   PRINT NM$, TOT
    250   WEND
    260   CLOSE #1

10. 300   OPEN "SALES" FOR INPUT AS #1
    310   READ PER$
    320   LET NM$ = "AAA"
    330   WHILE NM$ <> "ZZZ"

```
340          INPUT #1, NM$, TOT
350            IF NM$ = PER$ THEN PRINT NM$, TOT
360        WEND
370        CLOSE #1
380        DATA  LOCKE
```

In exercises 11 and 12, give the content of the file UPDATE after each program segment is executed. Assume that the contents of ORIGINAL at the beginning of each run are

```
"A",25<CR>"C",20<CR>"E",15<CR>"Z",0<CR><EOF>
```

11.
```
200        OPEN "ORIGINAL" FOR INPUT AS #1
210        OPEN "UPDATE" FOR OUTPUT AS #2
220        INPUT #1, L$, N
230        WHILE L$ <> "Z"
240          IF L$ <> "C" THEN WRITE #2, L$, N
250          INPUT #1, L$,N
260        WEND
270        CLOSE #1,#2
```

12.
```
300        OPEN "ORIGINAL" FOR INPUT AS #1
310        OPEN "UPDATE" FOR OUTPUT AS #2
320        READ Q$, P
330        LET L$ = ""
340        WHILE L$ <> "Z"
350          INPUT #1, L$, N
360          IF Q$ < L$ THEN WRITE #2, Q$, P
370          WRITE #2, L$, N
380        WEND
390        CLOSE #1, #2
400        DATA  D, 90
```

13. What statements should be added to the end of the program segment in exercise 11 to rename the file UPDATE as ORIGINAL?

PROGRAMMING PROBLEMS

1. Write a program that displays (in columns on the screen) the contents of a file called PAYROLL with records of the form NUM, NM$, RATE and terminated by 999,"*",0.

2. Suppose the PAYROLL file of problem 1 has no sentinel record. Write a program to display its contents using the EOF function.

Problems 3–6 refer to the following situation. René Descartes teaches French at Polytechnic High School. He would like to have a program—a sort of electronic grade sheet—to help him manage his students' grades. The grade sheet would be contained on a file called GRADES with records of the form

    student name, test 1 score, test 2 score, test 3 score

The records would be ordered by student name and terminated by "ZZZ",0,0,0. Only the last names of the students would appear in the file and each test score would be a number from 0 to 100.

3. Write a program that inputs the names of the students in any order from the user and creates the file GRADES in which they are listed in alphabetical order (ending with ZZZ). This program should also initialize all test scores in the file to 0.

4. Write a program that, at the option of the user, displays the entire contents of the file GRADES or just the record of a specified student. In either case, the student average(s) should also be displayed.

5. Write a program that allows the user to add a new student to the file GRADES or delete a student from this file.

6. Write a program that inputs from the user all student scores on a specified test and writes them to the file GRADES. This program should display the student names, one at a time, so that the user can enter the corresponding score.

7. Incorporate the programs in problems 3–6 into a single menu-driven program that performs the same functions.

8. Write programs to solve the following programming problems from previous chapters using (external) sequential files rather than (internal) DATA statements:

    a. chapter 5, problem 4   b. chapter 5, problem 6
    c. chapter 6, problem 5   d. chapter 7, problem 8

EDITING A BASIC PROGRAM

Editing a program is the process of making modifications in it for any reason (error-related or not). We will describe simple ways to edit a BASIC program; these methods should work on any computer system. Most computers have more sophisticated editing procedures which will save you time in the long run. Check your computer manual or consult with your instructor for more information about these procedures.

Correcting a Line before It Is Entered

If you make a typing mistake and you notice it before you press the Enter key, you can easily correct it. First, erase what you typed after the mistake (in reverse order) by successively pressing the Backspace key. Then press the Backspace key once more to erase the mistake. Finally, retype the rest of the line correctly. For example, suppose you want to type the line

```
200    PRINT "HELLO"
```

but instead you type

```
200    PRIT "H─ ◄─────── cursor
```

and notice that you've misspelled PRINT. To correct this error, press Backspace four times in succession erasing the H, then the ", then the blank, and finally the T. At this point, we have

```
200    PRI—  ◄────────── cursor
```

Now just type the rest of the line correctly.

NOTE   Depending on the keyboard, the Backspace key may be labeled "Backspace", "←", or "Delete". On some computers, you may have to hold down the Control key and press H to get the effect of a backspace.

Modifying Code after It Has Been Entered

Modifying a Program Line   To change a specific line in the program in memory, just retype the entire line (including the line number) and press the Enter key. The new line will replace the old one.

EXAMPLE A.1   Suppose that you have typed the code

```
190    PRINT "THIS IS A GOOD PROGRAM!"
200    PRINT "LET'S SEE HOW IT WORKS."
—  ◄────────── cursor
```

and you want to change the word GOOD (in line 190) to GREAT. You can do this by typing

```
190    PRINT "THIS IS A GREAT PROGRAM!"
```

On the screen, you will see

```
190    PRINT "THIS IS A GOOD PROGRAM!"
200    PRINT "LET'S SEE HOW IT WORKS."
190    PRINT "THIS IS A GREAT PROGRAM!"
```

In the computer's memory, however, the second occurrence of line 190 completely replaces the first. (To check this, just LIST your program.)

Deleting a Program Line   To delete a line from the program in memory, just type its line number and press the Enter key.

EXAMPLE A.2   Suppose the program in memory contains the code

```
350    PRINT "THIS IS A GOOD PROGRAM."
360    PRINT "NAY, A GREAT ONE!"
370    PRINT "I'M SURE YOU WILL AGREE."
```

To delete line 360, all you need do is type

```
360
```

and press the Enter key. When the program is listed, this segment of code will appear as

```
350    PRINT "THIS IS A GOOD PROGRAM."
370    PRINT "I'M SURE YOU WILL AGREE."
```

Inserting a Program Line   To insert a line into your program between lines n and m, type the new line using a line number that lies between n and m. Then press the Enter key.

EXAMPLE A.3   Suppose that your program contains the code

```
500    LET A = 5
510    LET C = A — B
```

To insert the statement LET B = 61.3 between these two, type

```
505    LET B = 61.3
```

and press the Enter key. (Of course, any line number between 500 and 510 would do just as well.) A listing of the program will show the code

```
500    LET A = 5
505    LET B = 61.3
510    LET C = A — B
```

EXPONENTIAL NOTATION

In applications, we sometimes encounter very large or very small numbers, such as 1,502,000,000 or 0.00000571. These numbers can be represented in a more manageable form using *scientific notation*. Here, the given number is represented as a value between 1 and 10 multiplied by the appropriate power of 10. For example,

$$1{,}502{,}000{,}000 = 1.502 \times 10^9 \text{ and } 0.00000571 = 5.71 \times 10^{-6}.$$

The BASIC equivalent of scientific notation is called **exponential notation.** In BASIC, instead of writing "10 to a power," we use the letter E followed by the given power. For example, 1.502×10^9 is written as 1.502E9, and 5.71×10^{-6} as $5.71E-6$. Additional examples are given in table B.1.

TABLE B.1   EXAMPLES OF EXPONENTIAL NOTATION

NUMBER	SCIENTIFIC NOTATION	EXPONENTIAL NOTATION
$-3{,}140{,}000$	-3.14×10^6	$-3.14E6$ or $-3.14E+6$
0.000000006	6×10^{-9}	$6E-9$
7.30	7.30×10^0	$7.3E0$

As shown in example B.1, the computer will automatically display numbers in exponential notation when they are very large or very small. (How large or small depends upon the version of BASIC you are using.)

EXAMPLE B.1   One light year is the distance that light travels in a year. Using the facts that light travels 186,000 miles per second, and there are 3,600 seconds in an hour, 24 hours in a day, and 365 days in a year, we can compute the equivalent of one light year in miles by means of the following program segment:

```
200        LET DIST = 186000 * 3600 * 24 * 365
210        PRINT "ONE LIGHT YEAR IN MILES: "; DIST
```

When these statements are executed, the number computed (DIST) is so large that it is automatically displayed in exponential notation.

```
ONE LIGHT YEAR IN MILES:   5.865696E+12
```

If a number is displayed in exponential notation, you can convert it into ordinary notation by simply moving the decimal point the number of places indicated by the integer following the *E*. If this integer is positive, move the decimal point to the right; if it is negative, move it to the left.

For example, given $1.67E-4$, we write down 1.67 and move the decimal point four places to the left.

$$0\,0\,0\,1.6\,7$$

Thus, $1.67E-4 = .000167$. To convert 4.2E5, we move the decimal point five places to the right.

$$4.2\,0\,0\,0\,0$$

getting 420000 or, as it is usually written, 420,000.

ANSWERS TO SELECTED REVIEW EXERCISES

INTRODUCTION

3. None of these are computers.

5. Central processing unit, primary storage (internal memory), secondary storage, input devices, and output devices.

7. Primary storage holds data immediately before and after they are used in the CPU, and it can be accessed at relatively high speed. However, the data in primary storage are lost when power is turned off, whereas data in secondary storage can be stored permanently, if so desired.

9. Machine languages, assembly languages, and high-level languages.

CHAPTER 1

1. a. 230   b. LET   c. X, A, B   d. 1

3. a. 21.00   .0   −7.3   +5.1   **5.** a. −2.333333   b. 9   c. 18

   b. A1   Q

7. 210   LET W = 21.8
    220   LET A = L * W
    230   PRINT "THE AREA IS"; A

9. 120   LET A = 14.2
    122   LET B = 121
    124   LET C = 7
    130   LET X = (A + B + C) / 3
    140   PRINT X
    150   END

11. WELCOME TO THIS PROGRAM.   **13.**   14
     IT DOES NOTHING.   9   4
                                          Y 3

CHAPTER 2

1. a. Q1$ and Q$ are valid   b. "HELLO"," ", and "1" are valid
      string variable names.   string constants.

3. b. and c. are valid BASIC statements.   **5.** 210   PRINT A, C
                                          220   PRINT B, D
                                          230   DATA 3, 5, 7, 9

7. X: 14.3   **9.** 123456789 123456789
     Y:JOE   GO GO
                                                       15.7

11. $4,321.60
     27.5
     V = 21.480 AND V + 3 = 24.48

13. 200   PRINT TAB(6) "NAME" TAB(20) "RANK" TAB(29) "SERIAL NUMBER"

CHAPTER 3

1. a. true   b. true   c. false   d. false

3. c.

5. a. Interchange the statements in lines 330 and 340.
     b. Insert:

        425   NEXT X

7. The errors are that the sentinel value is added to the sum and the formula for the average is not correct. The segment can be corrected as follows:

```
110    LET S = 0
120    LET C = 0
130    INPUT "ENTER A NUMBER ", N
140    WHILE N <> -99999
150       LET C = C + 1
160       LET S = S + N
170       INPUT "ENTER A NUMBER ", N
180    WEND
190    LET A = S / C
200    PRINT "AVERAGE:   "; A
```

9. 7 9 11

11. 10
     7
     4
     1
     -2

13. ENTER N
     ENTER N
     -5

15. a.
```
200    LET N = 10
210       PRINT N
220       LET N = N - 3
230    IF N >= 0 THEN 210
240    PRINT N
```

b.
```
200    LET N = 1
210    WHILE N > 0
220       INPUT "ENTER N ", N
230    WEND
240    PRINT N
```

CHAPTER 4

1. a. true   b. false

3. b.

5. This can be done using ON...GOTO, but is much easier with

```
400    IF X < 0 THEN PRINT "-1"
410    IF X = 0 THEN PRINT "0"
420    IF X > 0 THEN PRINT "1"
```

7. Delete line number 510.

9. a. 1
       11

b. 2
     -11

11. a. 1 IS SMALL

b. 1 IS OK

CHAPTER 5

1. b.

3. c.

5. Insert the following lines:

```
135      STOP
205      RETURN
305      RETURN
405      RETURN
```

7.
```
TWO
THREE
ONE
Break in 230
```

9. IS FUN?

CHAPTER 6

1. a. 13   b. 66   **3.** a. true   b. true

5. Insert line 525 and replace lines 540 and 550 as follows:

```
525          LET TEMP = HOG(K)
540          LET HOG(K+1) = TEMP
550          LET FLAG = 0
```

7. Substitute the following line: **9.** 3   1

```
660     LET AVG = SUM / N
```

11.
```
1   0   0
0   1   0
0   0   1
```

CHAPTER 7

1. a. 3.25   b. −1   c. −3

3. a. 0   b. the number e c. 1

5. d.

7. a. "TO"   b. "O E"   c. "VINE"   d. 18

9. a. "1"   b. "#"   c. 90   d. 70

11. a. false   b. true   c. true

13. a. DEF FNROUND(X) = FIX(100*X + SGN(X)*.5) / 100
b. DEF FNAVG(X,Y,Z) = (X + Y + Z) / 3
c. DEF FNAREA(B,H) = B * H / 2

15. Convert ANGLE to radians as follows:

```
625         LET ANGLE = ANGLE * 3.1416 / 180
```

17. Change the following lines:

```
510         LET K = 1
540         IF MID$(PHRASE$,N,1) = " " THEN LET K = K + 1
```

19. AG

21. a. 200   `DEF FNONE$(TEXT$,K) = MID$(TEXT$,K,1)`

    b. 210   `DEF FNTWO$(N$) = LEFT$(N$,1) + MID$(N$,INSTR(N$," ")+1,1)`

CHAPTER 8

1. a. true   b. true   c. true

3. a. true   b. false   c. true

5. a. 200   `OPEN "FILE1" FOR OUTPUT AS #1`

    b. 250   `WRITE #2, A, B, C`

    c. 300   `KILL "FILE3"`

7. Change:

```
200         OPEN "WRONG" FOR OUTPUT AS #1
260         PRINT K
```

    Insert:

```
233         CLOSE #1
236         OPEN "WRONG" FOR INPUT AS #1
```

9.
```
BURTON          12360
LOCKE           10580
POST            14120
```

11. `"A",25<CR>"E",15<CR><EOF>`

13.
```
280         KILL "ORIGINAL"
290         NAME "UPDATE" AS "ORIGINAL"
```

INDEX